content

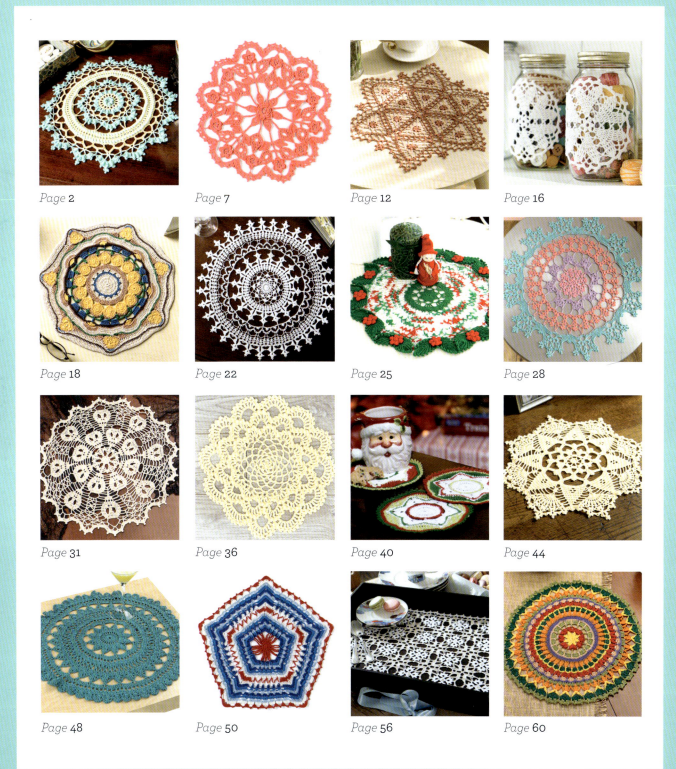

Page 2

Page 7

Page 12

Page 16

Page 18

Page 22

Page 25

Page 28

Page 31

Page 36

Page 40

Page 44

Page 48

Page 50

Page 56

Page 60

MW01505357

coventry doily

Experienced

MATERIALS

Yarn
• AUNT LYDIA'S® Crochet Thread, Size 10
• 1 ball each in 450 Aqua (A), 423 Maize (B), and 428 Mint Green (C)

Hook
• Steel crochet hook, size 7 (1.50mm), *or size to obtain gauge*

Notions
• Stitch marker
• Thread needle

FINISHED MEASUREMENTS

Approximately 12"/30.5cm in diameter

GAUGE

Rounds 1–4 = 1¾"/4.5cm across.
CHECK YOUR GAUGE.
Use any size hook to obtain gauge.

SPECIAL STITCHES

2-dc Cl (2 double crochet cluster) [Yarn over, insert hook in indicated stitch or space, yarn over and pull up loop, yarn over, draw through 2 loops on hook] twice, yarn over, draw through all 3 loops on hook.

3-dc Cl (3 double crochet cluster) [Yarn over, insert hook in indicated stitch or space, yarn over and pull up loop, yarn over, draw through 2 loops on hook] 3 times, yarn over, draw through all 4 loops on hook.

5-dc Cl (5 double crochet cluster) [Yarn over, insert hook in indicated stitch or space, yarn over and pull up loop, yarn over, draw through 2 loops on hook] 5 times, yarn over, draw through all 6 loops on hook.

2-tr Cl (2 treble crochet cluster) *[Yarn over] twice, insert hook in indicated stitch or space, yarn over and draw up a loop, [yarn over and draw through 2 loops on hook] twice; repeat from * once more, yarn over and draw through all 3 loops on hook.

4-tr popcorn Work 4 tr in indicated stitch or space, drop loop from hook, insert hook (from front to back) in first tr of the 5 tr just made, return dropped loop to hook and draw through.

dtr2tog-over-picots (double treble crochet 2 picots together) *[Yarn over] 3 times, insert hook in ch-4 space of next picot, yarn over and draw up a loop, [yarn over and draw through 2 loops on hook] 3 times; repeat from * once more, yarn over and draw through all 3 loops on hook. **Note** Skip all stitches between the two picots being joined with the dtr2tog.

ch-4 picot (chain-4 picot) Ch 4, slip stitch in top of last stitch made.

triple-picot Ch 4, slip stitch in front loop at top and front strand of actual stitch of last stitch made, ch 5, slip stitch in the same stitch catching front loop of first ch-4 loop where you slip stitched into top of stitch, ch 4, slip stitch in the same stitch catching front loop of first ch-4 loop and ch-5 loop where you slip stitched into top of stitch.

NOTES

1) Doily is worked in joined rounds with the right side always facing.

2) When instructed to join new yarn you may join using any method you choose (e.g. with a slip st, by simply drawing up a loop).

DOILY

With A, ch 4; join with slip st in first ch to form a ring.

Round 1 (Right Side) Ch 1, 8 sc in ring; join with slip st in front loop of first sc—8 sc.

Round 2 Ch 2, working in front loops only, (5-dc Cl, ch 3, slip st) in same st as joining, (slip st, ch 2, 5-dc Cl, ch 3, slip st) in each of next 7 sc—8 clusters. Fasten off and weave in ends.

Round 3 With right side facing, working behind clusters of Round 2 and into sts of Rounds 1, join C in back loop of any sc of Round 1, working in back loops only, ch 2, tr in same sc (first ch-2 and tr count as first 2-tr Cl), ch 1, 2-tr Cl in same sc, *ch 1, (2-tr Cl, ch 1, 2-tr Cl) in next sc; repeat from * around, ch 1; join with slip st in top of first cluster—16 clusters and 16 ch-1 spaces. Fasten off and weave in ends.

Round 4 With right side facing, join B in any ch-1 space of Round 3, ch 1,

coventry doily

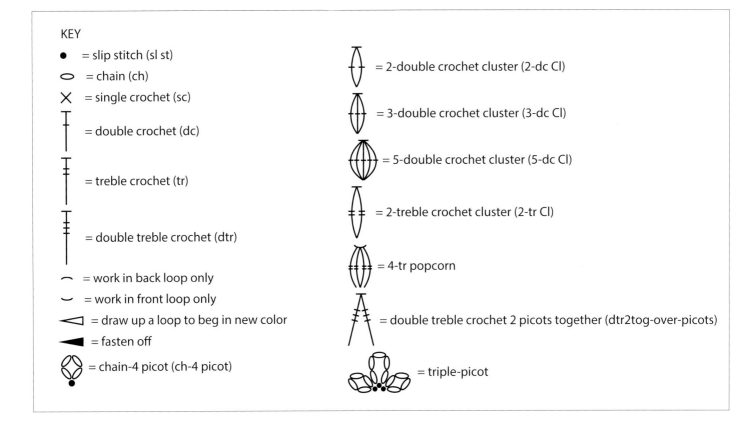

sc in same ch-1 space, *ch 5, sc in next ch-1 space; repeat from * around, ch 5; join with slip st in first sc—16 sc and 16 ch-5 spaces.

Round 5 (Slip st, ch 1, 2 sc, ch 2, 2 sc) in first ch-5 space, (2 sc, ch 2, 2 sc) in each of next 15 ch-5 spaces around; join with slip st in first sc—16 (2 sc, ch 2, 2 sc) groups. Fasten off and weave in ends.

Round 6 With right side facing, join A in any ch-2 space, ch 3 (counts as tr), (tr, 4-tr popcorn, ch-4 picot, 2 tr) in same ch-2 space, (2 tr, 4-tr popcorn, ch-4 picot, 2 tr) in each of next 15 ch-2 spaces around; join with slip st in top of beginning ch-3—Sixteen (2 tr, popcorn, picot, 2 tr) groups. Fasten off and weave in ends.

Round 7 With right side facing, join B in ch-4 space of any picot, ch 1, sc in same ch-4 space, *ch 7, sc in ch-4 space of next picot; repeat from * around, ch 7; join with slip st in first sc—16 sc and 16 ch-7 spaces.

Round 8 (Slip st, ch 1, 3 sc, ch 3, 3 sc) in first ch-7 space, (3 sc, ch 3, 3 sc) in each of next 15 ch-7 spaces; join with slip st in first sc—16 (3 sc, ch 3, 3 sc) groups. Fasten off and weave in ends.

Round 9 With right side facing, join C in any ch-3 space, ch 1, sc in same ch-3 space, ch 3, (tr, ch 3, tr, ch 4, tr, ch 3, tr) in next ch-3 space, * ch 3, sc in next ch-3 space, ch 3, (tr, ch 3, tr, ch 4, tr, ch 3, tr) in next ch-3 space; repeat from * around, ch 3; join with slip

st in first sc—8 (tr, ch 3, tr, ch 4, tr, ch 3, tr) groups, 8 sc, and 16 ch-3 spaces. Fasten off and weave in ends.

Round 10 With right side facing, join A in any sc, ch 2 (counts as dc), *skip next ch-3 space, (2 tr, 4-tr popcorn, ch-4 picot, 2 tr) in next ch-3 space, (tr, 4-tr popcorn, ch-4 picot, [tr, 4-tr popcorn, ch-4 picot] twice, tr) in next ch-4 space, (2 tr, 4-tr popcorn, ch-4 picot, 2tr) in next ch-3 space **, dc in next sc; repeat from * around ending last repeat at **; join with slip st in top of beginning ch—8 pattern repeats. Fasten off and weave in ends.

Round 11 With right side facing, join B in ch-4 space of 3rd picot, ch 12 (counts as dc, ch 10), skip next picot, dtr2tog-over-picots, *ch 10, skip next picot **, dc in next picot, ch 10, skip next picot, dtr2tog-over-picots; repeat from * around ending last repeat at **; join with slip st in 2nd ch of beginning ch-12—8 dtr2tog-over-picots, 8 dc and 16 ch-10 spaces.

Round 12 Ch 1, sc in same ch as joining, *11 sc in next ch-10 space, sc in space between the 2 legs of the next dtr2tog, 11 sc in next ch-10 space **, sc in next dc; repeat from * around ending last repeat at **; join with slip st in first sc—192 sc. Fasten off and weave in ends.

Round 13 With right side facing and working in back loops only, join C in first sc of previous round, ch 2 (counts as dc), 2-dc Cl in

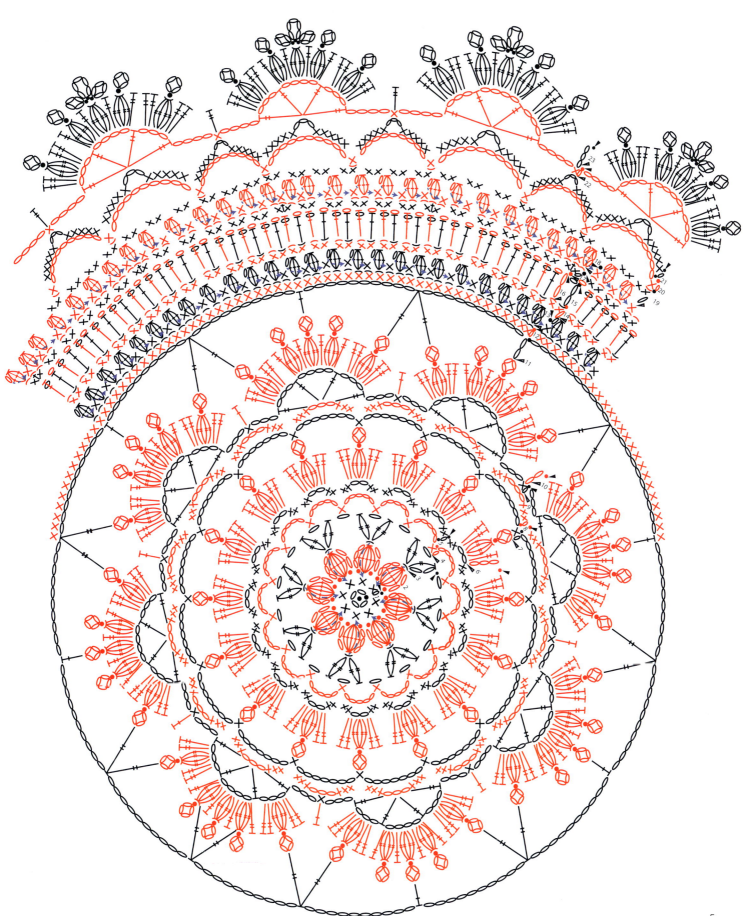

coventry doily

same sc, ch 1, working behind cluster just made, sc in last sc of previous round, *skip next unworked sc, 3-dc Cl in next sc, ch 1, working behind cluster just made, sc in skipped sc; repeat from * around; join with slip st in first sc—96 clusters, 96 sc, and 96 ch-1 spaces. Fasten off and weave in ends.

Round 14 With right side facing, join B in first sc, ch 1, 2 sc in same sc, 2 sc in each remaining sc around; join with slip st in front loop of first sc—192 sc.

Round 15 Ch 3 (counts as dc, ch 1), working in front loops only, skip next sc, dc in next sc, *ch 1, skip next sc **, dc in next sc; repeat from * around ending last repeat at **; join with slip st in 2nd ch of beginning ch—96 dc and 96 ch-1 spaces. Fasten off and weave in ends.

Round 16 With right side facing and working in back loops only, join A in first skipped sc, ch 3 (counts as dc, ch 1), dc in next skipped sc, *ch 1, dc in next skipped sc; repeat from * around, ch 1; join with slip st in 2nd ch of beginning ch-3—96 dc and 96 ch-1 spaces. Fasten off and weave in ends.

Note In Round 17, stitches are worked into ch-space/dc pairs. Each pair consists of a ch-1 space from Round 15 and a dc from Round 16. Insert the hook into the ch-space and the dc, then work the indicated stitches.

Round 17 With right side facing, join B by inserting hook in first ch-1 space of Round 15 and 2nd ch of beginning ch-3 of Round 16, ch 1, 3 sc in same ch/space pair, [2 sc in next ch-1 space of Round 15 and next dc of Round 16 at the same time] 5 times, * 3 sc in next ch-1 space of Round 15 and next dc of Round 16, [2 sc in next ch-1 space of Round 15 and next dc of Round 16] 5 times; repeat from * around; join with slip st in first sc—208 sc. Fasten off and weave in ends.

Round 18 Repeat Round 13—104 clusters, 104 sc, and 104 ch-1 sps. Fasten off and weave in ends.

Round 19 With right side facing, join B in sc of 2nd to last cluster of previous round, ch 1, 2 sc in same sc, 2 sc in each remaining sc around; join with slip st in front loop of first sc—208 sc.

Round 20 Slip st in next sc, ch 1, sc in same sc, ch 10, skip next 6 sc, sc in next sc, *ch 9, skip next 5 sc, sc in next sc, ch 10, skip next 6 sc, sc in next sc; repeat from * to last 5 sc, ch 9, skip last 5 sc; join with slip st in first sc—32 sc, 16 ch-9 spaces, and 16 ch-10 spaces. Place a marker in any one of the ch-9 spaces.

Round 21 Slip st in first ch-10 space, ch 1, (5 sc, ch 3, 5 sc) in same ch-space, (5 sc, ch 3, 5 sc) in each remaining ch-9 space and ch-10 space around; join with slip st in first sc—32 (5 sc, ch 3, 5 sc) groups. Fasten off and weave in ends.

Round 22 With right side facing, join C in the ch-3 space directly above the marked ch-9 space of Round 20, remove the marker, ch 1, sc in same ch-3 space, ch 4, (tr, [ch 4, tr] 3 times) in next ch-3 space, *ch 4, sc in next ch-3 space, ch 4, (tr, [ch 4, tr] 3 times) in next ch-3 space; repeat from * around, ch 4; join with slip st in first sc—16 (tr, [ch 4, tr] 3 times) groups. Fasten off and weave in ends.

Round 23 With right side facing, join A in first sc, ch 3 (counts as tr), *skip next ch-4 space, (2 tr, 4-tr popcorn, ch-4 picot, 2 tr) in next ch-4 space, (tr, 4-tr popcorn, ch-4 picot, 2 tr, 4-tr popcorn, triple-picot, 2 tr, 4-tr popcorn, ch-4 picot, tr) in next ch-4 space, (2 tr, 4-tr popcorn, ch-4 picot, 2 tr) in next ch-4 space **, tr in next sc; repeat from * around ending last repeat at **; join with slip st in top of beginning ch—16 pattern repeats. Fasten off and weave in ends.

FINISHING
Weave in any remaining ends. Block doily.●

AUNT LYDIA'S® Classic Crochet Thread, Size 10, Art. 154 available in white, ecru & natural 400yd/366m; solid color 350yd/320m; shaded color 300yd/274m balls.

exquisite flower doily

MATERIALS

Yarn
• AUNT LYDIA'S® Classic Crochet Thread, Size 10
• 1 ball 275 in Coral

Hook
• Steel crochet hook, size 7 (1.5mm), *or size to obtain gauge*

Notions
• Rust-proof pins
• Fabric stiffener
• Thread needle

FINISHED MEASUREMENTS

Approximately 14"/35.5cm in diameter

GAUGE

Small flower = approximately 1½"/4cm in diameter.
Small leaf = approximately 1x1½"/2.5x4cm.
CHECK YOUR GAUGE.
Use any size hook to obtain gauge.

SPECIAL STITCHES

join with sc Place a slip knot on hook, insert hook in indicated stitch, yarn over and draw up a loop, yarn over and draw through both loops on hook.
picot Ch 3, slip stitch in 3rd chain from hook.
puff Yarn over, insert hook in indicated stitch and draw up a loop, [yarn over, insert hook in same stitch and draw up a loop] 3 times, yarn over and draw through all 9 loops on hook.

SPECIAL TECHNIQUE

Adjustable Ring Wrap yarn into a ring, ensuring that the tail falls behind the working yarn. Grip ring and tail between middle finger and thumb. Insert hook through center of ring, yarn over (with working yarn) and draw up a loop. Work stitches of first round in the ring. After the first round of stitches is worked, pull gently on tail to tighten ring.

NOTES

1) Doily is made from 55 pieces that are worked separately. The pieces are arranged following Assembly Diagram then sewn together.
2) A border is worked around the outer edge of the joined pieces to finish doily.

CENTER FLOWER

Ch 6; slip st in first ch to form a ring.
Round 1 (Right Side) Ch 6 (counts as dc, ch 3), dc in ring, [ch 3, dc in ring] 4 times, ch 3; join with slip st in 3rd ch of beginning ch—6 dc and 6 ch-3 spaces.
Round 2 (Sc, hdc, 3 dc, hdc, sc) in each ch-3 space around; do not join—6 petals.
Round 3 Working behind petals, slip st around post of first dc of Round 1, *ch 5, slip st around post of next dc in Round 1; repeat from * 4 more

exquisite flower doily

times, ch 5; join with slip st in first slip st—6 ch-5 spaces.

Round 4 (Sc, hdc, 4 dc, hdc, sc) in each ch-5 space around; do not join—6 petals.

Round 5 Working behind petals, slip st around first dc in Round 1, *ch 7, slip st around post of next dc in Round 1; repeat from * 4 more times, ch 7; join with slip st in first slip st—6 ch-7 spaces.

Round 6 (Sc, hdc, 7 dc, hdc, sc) in each ch-7 space around; join with slip st in first sc—6 petals. Fasten off.

SMALL LEAF (make 6)

Make an adjustable ring.

Round 1 (Right Side) Ch 2 (does not count as a st), 10 hdc in ring; join with slip st in first hdc to join—10 hdc.

Round 2 Ch 4 (counts as tr), (tr, dc) in same st as joining, 2 hdc in next st, 2 sc in next st, 2 hdc in next st, (2 dc, tr) in next st, picot, (tr, 2 dc) in next st, 2 hdc in next st, 2 sc in next st, 2 hdc in next st, (dc, 2 tr) in next st; join with slip st in top of beginning ch—24 sts and 1 picot. Fasten off.

LACE LEAF I (make 6)

Ch 14; slip st in first ch to form a ring.

Round 1 (Right Side) Ch 1, 23 sc in ring; join with slip st in first sc—23 sc.

Round 2 Ch 1, sc in same st as joining, [ch 3, skip next st, hdc in next st] 4 times, ch 3, skip next st, dc in next st, ch 3, skip next st, (tr, ch 6, tr) in next st, ch 3, skip next st, dc in next st, [ch 3, skip next st, hdc in next st] 4 times, ch 3; join with slip st in first sc—13 sts, 12 ch-3 spaces, and 1 ch-6 space. Do not fasten off.

Round 3 Ch 16 (for stem), sc in 2nd ch from hook and in next 14 ch, 4 sc in each of first 6 ch-3 spaces, (4 sc, ch 2, 4 sc) in next ch-6 space, 4 sc in each of next 6 ch-3 spaces; join with slip st in first sc. Fasten off.

SINGLE STEM (make 6)

Ch 28.

Row 1 (Right Side) Sc in 2nd ch from hook and in next 9 ch, puff in next st, sc in next 16 ch—26 sc and 3 puffs.

SHORT ROW LEAF (make 12)

Ch 9.

Round 1 (Right Side) Sc in 3rd ch from hook (2 skipped ch count as beginning ch-2 space) and in next 5 ch, (sc, 3 hdc, sc) in last ch; working across opposite side of foundation ch, sc in next 6 ch, 3 sc in beginning ch-2 space; do not join—20 sts.

Row 2 Do not turn, sc in next 5 sc; leave remaining sts unworked.

Row 3 Ch 1, turn, working in front loops only, sc in first 6 sts, 3 sc in next st, sc in next 6 sts; leave remaining sts unworked.

Row 4 Ch 1, turn, working in back loops only, sc in first 7 sts, 3 sc in next st, sc in next 5 sts; leave remaining sts unworked.

Row 5 Ch 1, turn, working in front loops only, sc in first 6 sts, 3 sc in next st, sc in next 6 sts. Fasten off.

LACE LEAF II (make 12)

Ch 14; slip st in first ch to form a ring.

Rounds 1 and 2 Work same as Rounds 1 and 2 of Lace Leaf I. Do not fasten off.

Round 3 Ch 7 (for stem), sc in 2nd ch from hook and in next 5 ch, 4 sc in first 6 ch-3 spaces, (4 sc, ch 2, 4 sc) in next ch-6 space, 4 sc in each of next 6 ch-3 spaces; join with slip st in first sc. Fasten off.

SMALL FLOWER (make 12)

Ch 6; slip st in first ch to form a ring.

Rounds 1–4 Work same as Rounds 1–4 of Center Flower; join end of Round 4 with slip st in first sc. Fasten off.

ASSEMBLY

Arrange pieces following Assembly Diagram. Whipstitch pieces together. Sew just a few stitches where the pieces touch and carefully weave in ends.

BORDER

Round 1 (Right Side) With right side facing, join thread with sc in center st of top petal of any Small Flower, ch 20, sc in st near middle of side edge of next Lace Leaf II, *ch 20, sc in center st of top petal of next Small Flower, ch 20, sc in st near middle of side edge of next Lace Leaf II; repeat from * around, ch 20; join with slip st in first sc—24 ch-20 spaces and 24 sc.

Round 2 Ch 3 (counts as dc), 27 dc in first ch-20 space, *dc in next sc, 27 dc in next ch-20 space; repeat from * around; join with slip st in top of beginning ch—672 dc.

Round 3 Ch 3 (counts as dc), (dc, picot, 2 dc) in same st as joining, *ch 1, skip next 6 sts, (2 dc, picot, 2 dc) in next st; repeat from * to last 6 sts, ch 1, skip next 6 sts; join with slip st in top of beginning ch—96 picot. Fasten off.

FINISHING

Weave in any remaining ends.
Block.
Apply fabric stiffener following instructions on container. Pin out doily and allow to dry. ●

AUNT LYDIA'S® Classic Crochet Thread, Size 10, Art. 154 available in white, ecru, & natural 400yd/366m; solid color 350yd/320m; shaded color 300yd/274m balls.

exquisite flower doily

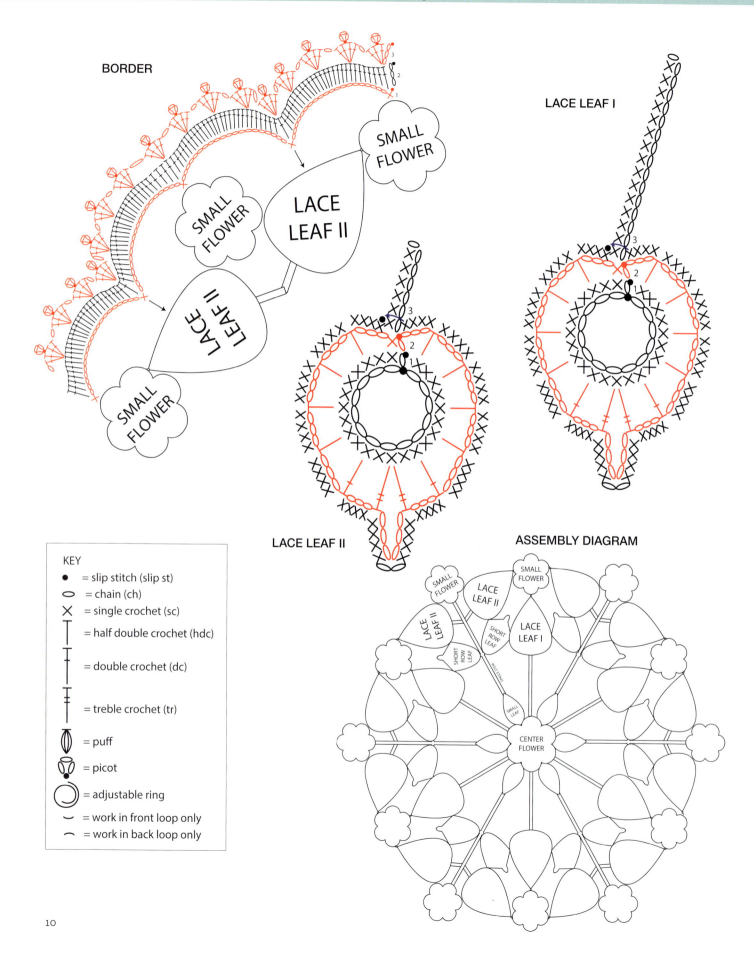

BORDER

LACE LEAF I

SMALL FLOWER

LACE LEAF II

SMALL FLOWER

LACE LEAF II

SMALL FLOWER

LACE LEAF II

KEY
- • = slip stitch (slip st)
- ⬭ = chain (ch)
- ✕ = single crochet (sc)
- | = half double crochet (hdc)
- ┬ = double crochet (dc)
- = treble crochet (tr)
- = puff
- = picot
- = adjustable ring
- = work in front loop only
- = work in back loop only

ASSEMBLY DIAGRAM

SMALL FLOWER

LACE LEAF II

SMALL FLOWER

LACE LEAF II

SHORT ROW LEAF

LACE LEAF I

SHORT ROW LEAF

SMALL LEAF

CENTER FLOWER

CENTER FLOWER

SMALL LEAF

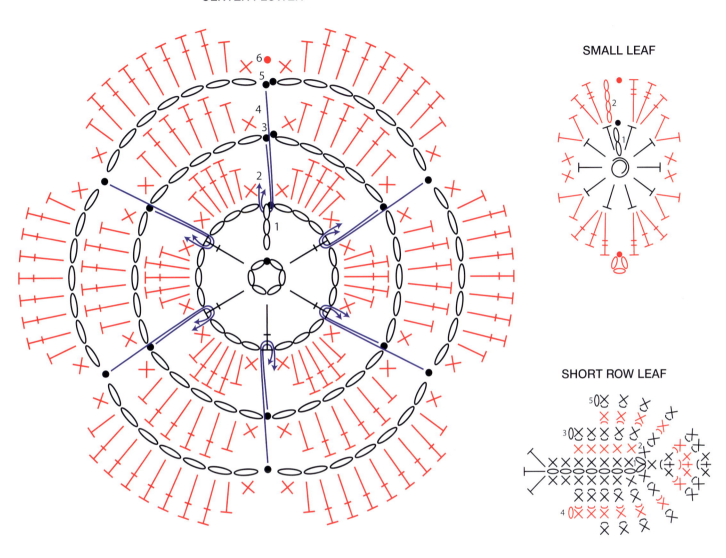

SHORT ROW LEAF

SINGLE STEM

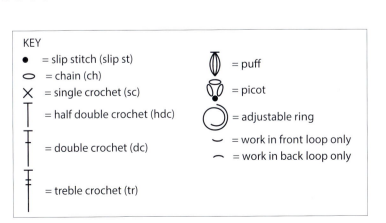

SMALL FLOWER

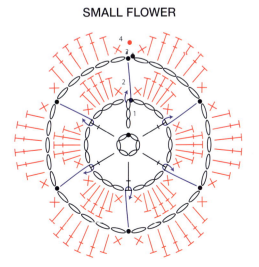

KEY

● = slip stitch (slip st)

◯ = chain (ch)

✕ = single crochet (sc)

┬ = half double crochet (hdc)

╪ = double crochet (dc)

⚊ = treble crochet (tr)

⬮ = puff

⬯ = picot

◯ = adjustable ring

⌣ = work in front loop only

⌢ = work in back loop only

fairfax doily

Experienced

MATERIALS

Yarn
• AUNT LYDIA'S® Classic Crochet Thread, Size 10
• 1 ball each in 341 Russet (A) and 310 Copper Mist (B)

Hook
• Steel crochet hook, size 7 (1.5mm), *or size to obtain gauge*

Notions
• Tapestry needle

FINISHED MEASUREMENTS
Approximately 16½"/42cm in diameter

GAUGE
Motif #1 = 3½"/9cm across.
CHECK YOUR GAUGE.
Use any size hook to obtain gauge.

SPECIAL ABBREVIATIONS

beg puff st (beginning puff st) Draw up a loop the height of a dc, [yarn over, insert hook into indicated stitch or space, draw up a loop the height of a dc] 5 times, yarn over, draw through all 11 loops on hook, ch 1 to close stitch.

puff st [Yarn over, insert hook into indicated stitch or space, draw up a loop the height of a dc] 6 times, yarn over, draw through all 13 loops on hook, ch 1 to close stitch.

4-tr cl (4-treble crochet cluster) Holding the last loop of each st on the hook, 2 tr in same ch-4 space, 2 tr in next ch-4 space, yarn over, draw through all 5 loops on hook.

4-dc cl (4-double crochet cluster) Holding the last loop of each st on the hook, 2 dc in same ch-4 space, 2 dc in next ch-4 space, yarn over, draw through all 5 loops on hook.

5-dc cl (5-double crochet cluster) Holding the last loop of each st on the hook, 2 dc in same ch-4 space, 3 dc in next ch-4 space, yarn over, draw through all 6 loops on hook.

ch-3 picot Ch 3, slip st in top of indicated st.

ch-4 picot Ch 4, slip st in top of indicated st.

etr (extended treble crochet) Yarn over twice, insert hook into indicated stitch or space, yarn over and pull up a loop (4 loops on hook), yarn over and draw through 1 loop on hook (4 loops on hook), [yarn over and draw through 2 loops on hook] 3 times.

joining picot Ch 1, slip st in next picot on adjoining Motif, ch 1, slip st in top of last dc made.

2-tr joining Holding the last loop of each st on the hook, tr in next ch-5 space on current Motif, tr in next ch-5 space on next outside Motif, yarn over, draw through all 3 loops on hook.

triple picot Ch 4, slip st in top of last stitch made, ch 5, slip st in the same st again catching the front loop of the first ch-4 loop, ch 4, slip st in the same st again catching the front loop of the first ch-4 loop and ch-5 loop.

dtr (double treble crochet Yarn over 3 times, insert hook into indicated stitch or space, yarn over and pull up a loop (5 loops on hook), [yarn over and draw through 2 loops on hook] 4 times.

dtr joining Holding the last loop of each st on the hook, dtr in next sc, skip next 9 sc, dtr in next sc, yarn over, draw through all 3 loops on hook,

NOTE
Motifs are joined as they are worked. To make finishing easier, weave in all ends as each section of each Motif is completed.

DOILY
Motif #1 (Beginning Motif in Center Section)
With A, ch 5; join with slip st in first ch to form a ring.
Round 1 (Right Side) Ch 1, [sc in ring, ch 2] 6 times; join with slip st in first sc—6 sc, 6 ch-2 loops.
Round 2 Slip st in first ch-2 space, beg puff st in same ch-2 space, *ch 4, puff st in next ch-2 space; repeat from * around; ch 4, slip st in top of beg puff st. Fasten off and weave in ends.

fairfax doily

Round 3 With Right Side facing, attach B in any ch-4 space, *ch 3, 4-tr cl, ch-4 picot in top of cluster just made, ch 4, slip st in same ch-4 space, ch 2, 4-dc cl, ch-4 picot in top of cluster just made, ch 3, slip st in same ch-4 space; repeat from * once, ch 3, 4-tr cl, ch-4 picot in top of cluster just made, ch 4, slip st in same ch-4 space, ch 2, 5-dc cl, ch 1, dc in top of cluster just made to form final picot.

Round 4 Ch 1, sc in picot just made, *ch 5, etr between clusters in next ch-4 space of Round 2, ch 5, (tr, ch 7, tr) in next picot, ch 5, etr between clusters in next ch-4 space of Round 2, ch 5, sc in next picot; repeat from *, ch 5, etr between clusters in next ch-4 space of Round 2, ch 5, (tr, ch 7, tr) in next picot, ch 5, etr between clusters in next ch-4 space of Round 2, ch 5, slip st in first sc. Fasten off and weave in ends.

Round 5 Attach A in first sc of previous round, ch 5, slip st in 2nd ch from hook (counts as dc and picot), *ch 2, dc in next ch-5 space, ch 2, dc in next etr, ch-3 picot in last dc made, ch 2, dc in next ch-5 space, ch 2, dc in next tr, ch-3 picot in last dc made, ch 2, (dc, ch 2, puff st, ch 5, puff st, ch 2, dc) in next ch-7 space, ch 2, dc in next tr, ch-3 picot in last dc made, ch 2, dc in next ch-5 space, ch 2, dc in next etr, ch-3 picot in last dc made, ch 2, dc in next ch-5 space, ch 2**, dc in next sc, ch-3 picot in last dc made; repeat from * once, then repeat from * to **, slip st in 2nd ch of beginning ch-5. Fasten off and weave in ends.

Motif #2 (One-Sided Joining Motif in Center Section)
Rounds 1–4 Same as Motif #1.
Round 5 Attach A in first sc of previous round, ch 5, slip st in 2nd ch from hook (counts as dc and picot), ch 2, dc in next ch-5 space, ch 2, dc in next etr, ch-3 picot in last dc made, ch 2, dc in next ch-5 space, ch 2, dc in next tr, ch-3 picot in last dc made, ch 2, (dc, ch 2, puff st, ch 5, puff st, ch 2, dc) in next ch-7 space, ch 2, dc in next tr, ch-3 picot in last dc made, ch 2, dc in next ch-5 space, ch 2 dc in next etr, ch-3 picot in last dc made, ch 2, dc in next ch-5 space, ch 2, dc in next sc, ch-3 picot in last dc made, ch 2, dc in next ch-5 space, ch 2, dc in next etr, ch-3 picot in last dc made, ch 2, dc in next ch-5 space, ch 2, dc in next tr, ch-3 picot in last dc made, ch 2, (dc, ch 2, puff st) in next ch-7 space, ch 2, holding Wrong sides together slip st between puff sts in any ch-5 space on previous Motif, ch 2, (puff st, ch 2, dc) in same ch-7 space on current Motif, ch 2, dc in next tr, joining picot, ch 2, dc in next ch-5 space, ch 2, dc in next etr, joining picot, ch 2, dc in next ch-5 space, ch 2, dc in next sc, joining picot, ch 2, dc in next ch-5 space, ch 2, dc in next etr, joining picot, ch 2, dc in next

ch-5 space, ch 2, dc in next tr, joining picot, ch 2, (dc, ch 2, puff st) in next ch-7 space, ch 2, slip st between puff sts in next ch-5 space on previous Motif, ch 2 ,(puff st, ch 2, dc) in same ch-7 space on current Motif, ch 2, dc in next tr, ch-3 picot in last dc made, ch 2, dc in next ch-5 space, ch 2, dc in next etr, ch-3 picot in last dc made, ch 2, dc in next ch-5 space, ch 2, slip st in 2nd ch of beginning ch-5. Fasten off and weave in ends.

Motifs #3–5 (One-Sided Joining Motifs in Center Section)
Rounds 1–4 Same as Motif #1.
Round 5 Same as Motif #2, working the first slip st joining between puff sts in the ch-5 space of the first joining of previous Motif.

Motif #6 (Two-Sided Joining Motif in Center Section)
Rounds 1–4 Same as Motif #1.
Round 5 Attach A in first sc of previous round, ch 5, slip st in 2nd ch from hook (counts as dc and picot), ch 2, dc in next ch-5 space, ch 2, dc in next etr, ch-3 picot in last dc made, ch 2, dc in next ch-5 space, ch 2, dc in next tr, ch-3 picot in last dc made, ch 2, (dc, ch 2, puff st) in next ch-7 space, ch 2, holding Wrong sides together slip st between puff sts in the ch-5 space on outside edge of Motif #1 so current Motif will fit between Motifs #1 and #5, ch 2, (puff st, ch 2, dc) in same ch-7 space on current Motif, ch 2, dc in next tr, joining picot, ch 2, dc in next ch-5 space, ch 2, dc in next etr, joining picot, ch 2, dc in next ch-5 space, ch 2, dc in next sc, joining picot, ch 2, dc in next ch-5 space, ch 2, dc in next etr, joining picot, ch 2, dc in next ch-5 space, ch 2, dc in next tr, joining picot, ch 2, (dc, ch 2, puff st) in next ch-7 space, ch 2, slip st between puff sts in next ch-5 space on Motif #1, slip st between puff sts in next ch-5 space on Motif #5, ch 2, (puff st, ch 2, dc) in same ch-7 space on current Motif, ch 2, dc in next tr, joining picot to Motif #5, ch 2, dc in next ch-5 space, ch 2, dc in next etr, joining picot, ch 2, dc in next ch-5 space, ch 2, dc in next sc, joining picot, ch 2, dc in next ch-5 space, ch 2, dc in next etr, joining picot, ch 2, dc in next ch-5 space, ch 2, dc in next tr, joining picot, ch 2, (dc, ch 2, puff st) in next ch-7 space, ch 2, slip st between puff sts in next ch-5 space on Motif #5, ch 2, (puff st, ch 2, dc) in same ch-7 space on current Motif, ch 2, dc in next tr, ch-3 picot in last dc made, ch 2, dc in next ch-5 space, ch 2, dc in next etr, ch-3 picot in last dc made, ch 2, dc in next ch-5 space, ch 2, slip st in 2nd ch of beginning ch-5. Fasten off and weave in ends.

Motifs #7-12 (Point Motifs on outside of Center Section)
Attach one Motif to each outside edge of Motifs #1–6.

Rounds 1–4 Same as Motif #1.

Round 5 Same as Motif #2, working the first slip st joining between puff sts in the ch-5 space of the outside corner of a Motif in the center section.

EDGING

Round 1 With Right Side facing, attach A in the first dc without a picot at the bottom right of any outside Motif, ch 1, sc in same dc, [ch 7, skip dc with picot, sc in next dc] 5 times, (ch 7, sc, ch 7, sc) in next ch-5 space, ch 7, sc in next dc, [ch 7, skip dc with picot, sc in next dc] 5 times, ch 3, 2-tr joining, ch 3, *sc in next dc, [ch 7, skip dc with picot, sc in next dc] 5 times, (ch 7, sc, ch 7, sc) in next ch-5 space, ch 7, sc in next dc, [ch 7, skip dc with picot, sc in next dc] 5 times, ch 3, 2-tr-joining, ch 3; repeat from * around, slip st in beginning sc. Fasten off and weave in ends.

Round 2 Attach B in the first ch-7 space of Round 1, beg puff st, [ch 5, puff st in next ch-7 space] 6 times, ch 5, puff st in same space, [ch 5, puff st in next ch-7 space] 6 times, ch 1, *puff st in next ch-7 space, [ch 5, puff st in next ch-7 space] 6 times, ch 5, puff st in same space, [ch 5, puff st in next ch-7 space] 6 times, ch 1; repeat from * around, slip st in top of beginning puff st. Fasten off and weave in ends.

Round 3

Beginning Motif Point
Attach A in the ch-5 space on the tip of any Point, ch 1, (3 sc, ch-3 picot in last sc made, 3 sc, triple picot in last sc made, 3 sc, ch-3 picot in alast sc made, 2 sc) in same space.

Motif Side
*(4 sc, triple picot in last sc made, 3 sc) in next ch-5 space; repeat from * 3 times

Picot Trim Between Motifs
[7 sc in next ch-5 space] 2 times, 3 sc in next ch-1 space, 7 sc in next ch-5 space, 3 sc in next ch-5 space, ch 4 (counts as a st), turn; skip next 5 sc, dtr joining, ch 4, skip next 5 sc, sc in next sc, slip st in next sc, ch 1, turn; 5 sc in next ch-4 space, sc between the 2 dtr of dtr joining, 3 sc in next ch-4 space, ch 3 (counts as a st), turn; skip next 2 sc, (puff st, ch 3, puff st) in next sc, ch 3, skip next 2 sc, sc in next sc, slip st in next sc, ch 1, turn; (3 sc, ch-3 picot in last sc madc, 2 sc) in next ch-3 space, (3 sc, triple picot in last sc made, 2 sc) in next ch-3 space, (3 sc, ch-3 picot in

last sc made, 2 sc) in next ch-3 space, 2 sc in next ch-4 space, 4 sc in next ch-5 space.

Repeat Motif Side.

Motif Point
(3 sc, ch-3 picot in last sc made, 3 sc, triple picot in last sc made, 3 sc, ch-3 picot in last sc made, 2 sc) in next ch-5 space. Continue working Edging, repeating [Motif Side, Picot Trim Between Motifs, Motif Side, Motif Point] 4 times, then [Motif Side, Picot Trim Between Motifs, Motif Side] once; slip st in first sc of Beginning Motif Point. Fasten off and weave in ends. Block Doily to size and shape.●

AUNT LYDIA'S® Classic Crochet Thread, Size 10, Art. 154 available in white & ecru 400yd/366m; solid color 250yd/228; shaded color 300yd/274m balls.

heart's desire doily-ed jars

Easy

MATERIALS

Yarn
- AUNT LYDIA'S® Crochet Thread, Size 10
- 1 ball in 001 White

Hook
- Steel crochet hook, size 7 (1.5mm), *or size to obtain gauge*

Notions
- Smooth 7"/17.8cm high mason jar
- Clear-drying household glue

FINISHED MEASUREMENTS
Approximately 5 x 5"/12.5 x 12.5cm

SPECIAL ABBREVIATIONS

beg cl (beginning cl) [yo and draw up a loop, yo and draw through 2 loops] twice all in ring, yo and draw through all 3 loops on hook.

cl (cluster) [yo and draw up a loop, yo and draw through 2 loops] 3 times all in ring, yo and draw through all 4 loops on hook.

beg 5-dc-cl (worked over next 4 sts) [yo and draw up a loop in next dc, yo and draw through 2 loops] 4 times, yo and draw through all 5 loops on hook.

5-dc-cl (worked over next 5 sts) [yo and draw up a loop in next dc, yo and draw through 2 loops] 5 times, yo and draw through all 6 loops on hook.

picot ch 3, slip st in top and side loops of sc.

DOILY

Ch 7; join with a slip st to form a ring.

Round 1 Ch 2, beg cl, ch 4, [cl, ch 4] 5 times; join with a slip st to top of beg cl.

Round 2 Slip st in first 2 ch of ch-4, slip st into ch-space, ch 3, 2 dc in same space, ch 4, [3 dc in next ch-4 space, ch 4] 5 times; join to top of ch-3.

Round 3 Ch 3, dc in same ch as joining, *dc in next dc, 2 dc in next dc, ch 2, sc in ch-4 space, ch 2 **, 2 dc in next dc; repeat from * around, end at **; join.

Round 4 Ch 3, dc in same ch as joining, *dc in next 3 dc, 2 dc in next dc, ch 4 **, 2 dc in next dc; repeat from * around, end at **; join.

Round 5 Ch 3, dc in same ch as joining, *dc in next 5 dc, 2 dc in next dc, ch 2, sc in ch-4 space, ch 2 **, 2 dc in next dc; repeat from * around, end at **; join.

Round 6 Ch 3, dc in next 3 dc, *(dc, ch 4, dc) all in next dc, dc in next 4 dc, ch 4 **, dc in next 4 dc; repeat from * around, end at **; join.

Round 7 Ch 3, dc in next 4 dc, *ch 4, sc in next ch-4 space, ch 4, dc in next 5 dc, ch 2, sc in next ch-4 space, ch 2 **, dc in next 5 dc; repeat from * around, end at **; join.

Round 8 Ch 2, beg 5-dc-cl, *[ch 5, sc in next ch-4 loop] twice, ch 5, 5-dc-cl, ch 7 **; 5-dc-cl; repeat from * around, end at **; join to top of first cl.

Round 9 Ch 1, (3 sc, picot, 3 sc) all in ch-5 loop, *[(3 sc, picot, 3 sc) all in next loop] twice, (4 sc, picot, 4 sc) all in next ch-7 loop **, (3 sc, picot, 3 sc) all in next ch-5 loop; repeat from * around, end at **; join to first sc.
Fasten off. Weave in ends.

FINISHING
Lay the doily flat (right side down) and evenly rub with glue. Place on the center of the jar. Allow to dry completely before moving. ●

AUNT LYDIA'S® Classic Crochet Thread, Size 10, Art. 154 available in white & ecru 400yd/366m; solid color 350yd/320m; shaded color 300yd/274m balls.

sun blossom mandala doily

MATERIALS

Yarn
• AUNT LYDIA'S® Classic Crochet Thread, Size 10
• 1 ball each in 226 Natural (A), 805 Blue Hawaii (B), 310 Copper Mist (C), 422 Golden Yellow (D), 484 Myrtle Green (E), and 131 Fudge Brown (F)

Hook
• Crochet hook, size B-1 (2.25mm), *or size to obtain gauge*

Notions
• Size ¹/₅ darning needle (large eye, sharp point)
• 14 stitch markers

FINISHED MEASUREMENTS

Approximately 12"/30.5cm in diameter

GAUGE

Rounds 1–7 = 3½"/9cm in diameter.
Circle = 1"/2.5cm in diameter.
CHECK YOUR GAUGE.
Use any size hook to obtain gauge.

SPECIAL STITCHES

cluster Yarn over (twice), insert hook in designated space, yarn over, draw up a loop to the height of a dc, yarn over, draw through 2 loops on hook, [yarn over, draw up a loop in same space, yo, draw through 2 loops] twice (5 loops on hook), yarn over, draw through 4 loops, yarn over, draw through last 2 loops.
tr2tog *Yarn over (twice), insert hook in next st, draw up a loop, [yarn over, draw yarn through 2 loops on hook] twice; repeat from * once, yarn over, draw yarn through 3 loops on hook.

NOTE

Press mandala several times during construction to make it lay flat and show stitches clearly, especially after yellow circles and blossoms are added.

DOILY

With A, ch 3, join with slip st to form a ring.
Round 1 Ch 3 (counts as dc here and throughout), 14 dc in ring; join with a slip st in top of beginning ch-3—15 dc.
Round 2 Ch 3, dc in first st, 2 dc in each dc around; join with a slip st in top of beginning ch-3—30 dc.
Round 3 Ch 3, 2 dc in next dc, *dc in next dc, 2 dc in next dc; repeat from * around; join with a slip st in top of beginning ch-3—45 dc. Fasten off A.
Round 4 With right side facing, join B with slip st in any st, ch 2 (counts as hdc here and throughout), skip first st, hdc in each dc around; join with a slip st in top of beginning ch-2—45 hdc. Fasten off B.
Round 5 With right side facing, join A in any st, ch 3, 3 dc in same st, *[skip next 2 sts, 4 dc in next st] 3 times, skip next 3 sts, 4 dc in next st; repeat from * twice, skip next 2 sts, 4 dc in next st, skip next 2 sts; join with a slip st in top of beginning ch-3—56 dc; 14 4-dc groups. Fasten off A.
Round 6 With right side facing, join C in first dc, ch 2, skip first st, hdc in each of next 3 dc, dc in space before next dc, *hdc into next 4 dc, hdc in space before next dc; repeat from * around; join with a slip st in top of beginning ch-2—70 hdc.
Round 7 Ch 2, skip first st, hdc in each of next 3 sts, 2 hdc in next st, *hdc in each of next 4 sts, 2 hdc in next st; rep from * around; join with a slip st in top of beginning ch-2—84 hdc. Fasten off C.
Prepare round for attachment of circles by placing 14 stitch markers evenly spaced around. Line them up with the center of each 4-dc group from Round 5, leaving 4 sts between markers.

Round 8
First Circle
With D, leaving a 5"/12.5cm tail, ch 3, join with slip st to form ring.
Round 1 Ch 4 (counts as tr here and throughout), 19 tr in ring; join with a slip st in top of beginning ch-4, slip st in any marked st in Round 7, slip st in last st of Circle—20 tr. Fasten off D.

sun blossom mandala doily

Second through Thirteenth Circles
With D, leaving a 5"/12.5cm tail, ch 3, join with slip st to form a ring.
Round 1 Ch 4, 16 tr in ring, skip 4 sts to the left of last join in Round 7, slip st in next marked st, 3 tr in ring of current Circle, skip 3 sts on previous Circle to the left of joining, slip st in next tr; join with a slip st in top of beginning ch-4 of current Circle—20 tr. Fasten off D.

Fourteenth Circle
With D, leaving a 5"/12.5cm tail, ch 3, join with slip st to form ring.
Round 1 Ch 4, 11 tr in ring, skip 4 sts to the right of where First Circle is joined to Round 7, slip st in next tr on First Circle, 4 tr in center ring of current Circle, skip 4 sts to the left of last join in Round 7, slip st in next marked st, 4 tr in ring of current Circle, skip 3 sts on previous Circle to the left of joining, slip st in next tr; join with a slip st in top of beginning ch-4 of current Circle—20 tr. Fasten off D.

Round 9 With right side facing, skip 1 tr to the left of join between any 2 Circles in Round 8, join C in next tr, ch 2, skip first st, hdc in next st, sc in each of next 2 sts, 2 sc in next st, sc in each of next 2 sts, hdc in each of next 2 sts, *skip last st of current Circle and first st on next Circle, hdc in each of next 2 sts, sc in each of next 2 sts, 2 sc in next st, sc in each of next 2 sts, hdc in each of next 2 sts; repeat from * around; join with a slip st in top of beginning ch-2—140 sts. Fasten off C.
Round 10 With right side facing, skip 4 sts to the left of space between any 2 Circle, join E with a slip st in next sc in Round 9, ch 1, sc in same st, *ch 5, skip next 5 sts, work cluster in space between circles, ch 5, skip next 4 sts **, sc in next st; rep from * around, ending last repeat at **; join with a slip st in first sc—28 ch-5 loops. Fasten off E.
Round 11 With right side facing, join B in ch-5 loop to the left of any cluster, ch 4, 5 tr in same loop, ch 1, *6 tr in next loop, ch 5, skip next ch-5 loop, dc in next sc, ch 5, skip next ch-5 loop **, 6 tr in next loop, ch 1; repeat from * around, ending last repeat **; join with a slip st in top of beginning ch-4—14 ch-5 loops; 7 ch-1 spaces; 14 groups of 6-tr. Fasten off B.
Round 12 With right side facing, join F in ch-5 loop after any single dc, ch 1, *7 sc in ch-5 loop, hdc in each of next 6 tr, 2 dc in next ch-1 space, hdc in each of next 6 tr, 7 sc in next ch-5 loop; repeat from * around—198 sts. Fasten off F.
Round 13 (fan round) *With right side facing, locate space between 2 sc, centered over any single dc in Round 11, join D with a slip st in 3rd sc to the right, skip next 2 sc, work 6 dc in space before next sc (in space directly over dc in Round 11), skip next 2 sc, sl st in next sc, fasten off; repeat from * around—7 Fans.

Round 14 With right side facing, skip 1 sc to the left of last slip st made in any Fan, join C with a slip st in next st, ch 1, starting in same st, *sc in each of next 20 sts, leaving 1 st free before next Fan, ch 8, skip next Fan, skip next sc; repeat from * around—7 ch-8 loops. Fasten off C.
Round 15 (arch round) *With right side facing, join C with a slip st, 3 sts to the right of any ch-8 loop, do not ch, sc in next st, hdc in next st, 12 dc in next ch-8 loop, hdc in next st, sc in next st, slip st in next st, fasten off; repeat from * around—7 Arches.
Round 16 With right side facing, join A with a slip st last slip st of any Arch, ch 4, tr in each of next 15 sts, [dc in next 2 sts, 2 dc in next st, dc in next 3 sts, 2 dc in next st] twice, dc in next 2 sts **, tr in each of next 16 sts; repeat from * around, ending last repeat at **, join with a slip st in top of beginning ch-4—252 sts.
Round 17 With right side facing, join E with a slip st in first st, ch 1, sc loosely in each st around. Fasten off E.
Place 7 evenly spaced stitch markers around, placing 1 marker centered over each ch-1 space in Round 11 for 7 blossoms.

Round 18
Blossom (make 7)
Round 1 With D, ch 4 (counts as dc), 11 dc in 4th ch from hook; join with a slip st in top of beginning ch-4—12 dc.
Round 2 Do not ch, *skip next dc, 8 dc in next st, skip next dc, slip st in next dc; repeat from * twice—3 petals. Attach stitch marker to ending loop, so it can be brought back up later. Cut thread but do not fasten off.
Row 3 With right side facing, join C with a slip st in 5th st to the right of join, ch 1, sc in same st, sc in each of next 4 sts, sc in joining slip st, sc in next 5 sts. Fasten off C.

Joining Pull marked D loop up from Blossom Round 2, remove marker. Place D loop on hook, slip st in marked st in Round 17, slip st in top of beginning ch-4 of Round 1 of Blossom. Fasten off D.

Round 19 With right side facing, join C in first st to the left of last sc in Row 3 of any Blossom, ch 1, starting in same st, *[sc in next 5 sts, 2 sc in next st] twice, sc in next 4 sts, slip st in next sc in Row 3 of same Blossom, working in sts of Round 17, skip next 5 sts from joining of Blossom, [tr2tog over next 2 sts] twice, dc in next 2 sts, hdc in next 2 sts, sc in next 10 sts, hdc in next 2 sts, dc in next 2 sts, [tr2tog over next 2 sts] twice, starting in first st to the left of last sc in Row 3 of next Blossom; repeat from * around; join with a slip st in first sc. Fasten off C.
Round 20 With right side facing, *identify the 6 sc centered over the top of any Blossom, join B with slip st in sc before the 6 center sc, do not ch, sc in next 6 sts, slip st in next st, fasten off; repeat from * over top of each Blossom around.

wisteria doily

strands held together, *ch 3, (dc, [ch-3 picot, dc] 3 times) in next ch-2 space, ch 3, insert hook under both ch-6 strands from Rounds 3 and 4, (sc, ch 3, sc) over both strands held together; repeat from * 6 times, ch 1, hdc in second ch of ch-5 at beginning of Round (counts as ch-3).

Round 6 Ch 15, skip next shell of (dc, 3 ch-3 picots, dc), 2-tr joining worked over next 2 ch-3 spaces, *ch 12, skip next shell **, 2-tr joining worked over next 2 ch-3 spaces; repeat from * 5 times, then from * to ** once, tr in next ch-3 space, slip st in third ch of ch-15 at beginning of Round. Fasten off.

Round 7 Attach B between the 2 tr of any 2-tr joining, ch 1, sc in same space, *(7 sc, ch 2, 7 sc) in next ch-12 space **, sc between next 2-tr joining; repeat from * 6 times, then from * to ** once, slip st in first sc of Round.

Round 8 Ch 1, sc in same sc, sc in next 3 sc, *ch 2, skip next 4 sc, [3-tr cl, ch 2] 4 times in next ch-2 space, skip next 4 sc **, sc in next 7 sc; repeat from * 6 times, then from * to ** once, sc in next 3 sc, slip st in first sc of Round.

Round 9 Ch 1, (sc, ch-3 picot, sc) in same first sc, *ch 2, skip next 3 sc, sc in next ch-2 space, ch 2, Small Shell in next ch-2 space, Large Shell in next ch-2 space, Small Shell in next ch-2 space, ch 2, sc in next ch-2 space, ch 2, skip next 3 sc **, (sc, ch-3 picot, sc) in next sc; repeat from * 6 times, then from * to ** once, slip st in first sc of Round. Fasten off.

Round 10 Reattach B in ch-2 space of first Small Shell on Round 9, ch 10, *dc in ch-3 space of next Large Shell, ch 7, tr in ch-2 space of next Small Shell, ch 7 **, tr in ch-2 space of next Small Shell, ch 7; repeat from * 6 times, then from * to ** once, slip st in third ch of ch-10 at beginning of Round. Fasten off.

Round 11 Attach C in any ch-7 space, (ch 1, 4 sc, ch 3, 4 sc) in same space, *(4 sc, ch 3, 4 sc) in next ch-7 space; repeat from * around, slip st in first sc of Round.

Round 12 Ch 1, sc in same first sc, *ch 2, skip next 3 sc, (4-dc cl, ch 3, 4-dc cl) in next ch-3 space, ch 2, skip next 3 sc, sc in next sc, ch-3 picot **, sc in next sc; repeat from * around to last ch-3 space, then from * to ** once, slip st in first sc of Round.

Round 13 Slip st in first 2 chs and next 4-dc cl, (slip st, ch 2, dc, ch 2, 2 dc) in next ch-3 space, ch 7, *Small Shell in next ch-3 space, ch 7; repeat from * around, slip st in second ch at beginning of Round.

Round 14 Slip st in first dc, (slip st, ch 2, dc, ch 2, 2 dc) in next ch-2 space, ch 7, *Small Shell in next ch-2 space, ch 7; repeat from * around, slip st in second ch at beginning of Round.

Round 15 Slip st in first dc and ch-2 space, (ch 5, slip st in 4th ch from hook, dc, [ch-3 picot, dc] 2 times) in same ch-2 space, ch 4, insert hook under both ch-7 strands from Rounds 13 and 14, (sc, ch 3, sc) over both strands held together, *ch 4, (dc, [ch-3 picot, dc] 3 times) in next ch-2 space, ch 4, insert hook under both ch-7 strands from Rounds 13 and 14, (sc, ch 3, sc) over both strands held together; repeat from * around, ch 1, dc in second ch of ch-5 at beginning of Round (counts as ch-4).

Round 16 Ch 15, skip next shell of (dc, 3 ch-3 picots, dc), 2-dtr joining worked over next 2 ch-4 spaces, *ch 11, skip next shell **, 2-dtr joining worked over next 2 ch-4 spaces; repeat from * around to last shell, then from * to ** once, dtr in next ch-4 space, skip (sc, ch-4, sc), slip st in fourth ch of ch-15 at beginning of Round. Fasten off.

Round 17 Attach D between the 2 dtr of any 2-dtr joining, ch 2, *11 dc in next ch-11 space **, dc between next 2-dtr joining; repeat from * around to last 2-dtr joining, then from * to ** once, slip st in second ch at beginning of Round.

Round 18 Ch 1, sc in same st, sc in next 9 dc, *ch 5, skip next 5 dc **, sc in next 19 dc; repeat from * to last 14 sts, then from * to ** once, sc in next 9 dc, slip st in first sc of Round.

Round 19 Ch 1, sc in same sc, sc in next 5 sc, *ch 3, skip next 4 sc, [3-tr cl, ch 3] 4 times in next ch-5 space, skip next 4 sc **, sc in next 11 sc; repeat from * around to last ch-5 space, then from * to ** once, sc in next 5 sc, slip st in first sc of Round.

Round 20 Ch 1, sc in same sc, *skip next sc, sc in next 4 sc, 2 sc in next ch-3 space, ch 2, [Small Shell in next ch-3 space, ch 6] 2 times, Small Shell in next ch-3 space, ch 2, 2 sc in next ch-3 space, sc in next 4 sc, skip next sc **, sc in next sc; repeat from * around 10 times, then from * to ** once, slip st in first sc of Round.

Round 21 Ch 1, sc in same sc, *skip next sc, sc in next 5 sc, 2 sc in next ch-2 space, ch 2, [Small Shell in next ch-2 space, ch 7, skip next ch-6] 2 times, Small Shell in next ch-2 space, ch 2, 2 sc in next ch-2 space, sc in next 5 sc, skip next sc **, sc in next sc; repeat from * around 10 times, then from * to ** once, slip st in first sc of Round.

Round 22 Ch 1, (sc, triple picot, sc) in same sc, *skip next sc, sc in next 6 sc, 2 sc in next ch-2 space, ch 2; (dc, ch-3 picot, dc, picot-in-ch, ch 1, dc, ch-3 picot, dc) in next ch-2 space; ch 3, insert hook under ch-6 strand from Round 20 and ch-7 strand from Round 21, (sc, ch 3, sc) over both strands held together, ch 4; (dc, ch-3 picot, 2 dc, triple picot, 2 dc, ch-3 picot, dc) in next ch-2 space; ch 4, insert hook under ch-6 strand from Round 20 and ch-7 strand from Round 21, (sc, ch 3, sc) over both strands held together, ch 3; (dc, ch-3 picot, dc, picot-in-ch, ch 1, dc, ch-3 picot, dc) in next ch-2 space; ch 2, 2 sc in next ch-2 space, sc in next 6 sc, skip next sc **; (sc, triple picot, sc) in next sc; repeat from * around 10 times, then from * to ** once, slip st in first sc of Round. Fasten off and weave in ends. Block doily to size and shape. ●

AUNT LYDIA'S® Classic Crochet Thread, Size 10, Art. 154 available in white, ecru & natural 400yd/366m; solid color 350yd/320m; shaded color 300yd/274m balls.

skulduggery doily

MATERIALS

Yarn
- AUNT LYDIA'S® Fashion 3
- 2 balls in 926 Bridal White

Hook
- Crochet hook, size C-2 (2.75mm), *or size to obtain gauge*

Notions
- Yarn needle

FINISHED MEASUREMENTS

Approximately 19½"/49.5cm in diameter

GAUGE

Rounds 1–6 = 3½"/9cm in diameter.
CHECK YOUR GAUGE.
Use any size hook to obtain gauge.

SPECIAL STITCHES

dc2tog (double crochet 2 stitches together) [Yarn over, insert hook in next stitch, yarn over and pull up loop, yarn over, draw through 2 loops] 2 times, yarn over, draw through all 3 loops on hook.

dc3tog (double crochet 3 stitches together) [Yarn over, insert hook in next stitch, yarn over and pull up loop, yarn over, draw through 2 loops] 3 times, yarn over, draw through all 4 loops on hook.

Fpdc (Front post double crochet) Yarn over, insert hook from front side of work to back and to front again around post of indicated stitch, yarn over and pull up a loop (3 loops on hook), [yarn over and draw through 2 loops on hook] twice.

picot (chain-3 picot) Ch 3, slip stitch in top of last stitch made.

sc2tog (single crochet 2 stitches together [Insert hook in next stitch, yarn over and pull up a loop] twice, yarn over and draw through all 3 loops on hook.

tr2tog (treble crochet 2 stitches together) [Yarn over] twice, insert hook in first indicated stitch, yarn over and pull up a loop, [yarn over and draw through 2 loops] twice (first leg of tr2tog made – 2 loops remain on hook), [yarn over] twice, insert hook in 2nd indicated stitch, yarn over and pull up a loop, [yarn over and draw through 2 loops] twice (2nd leg of tr2tog made), yarn over and draw through all 3 loops on hook.

DOILY

Ch 5; join with slip st in first ch to form a ring.

Round 1 (Right Side) Ch 2 (counts as first dc here and throughout, unless otherwise noted), work 15 dc in ring; join with slip st in top of beginning ch-2—16 dc.

Round 2 Ch 1, sc in same dc as join, *sc in next dc, (sc, ch 3, sc) in next dc; repeat from * to last dc, sc in last dc, sc again in same dc as join; join with ch

1, hdc in first sc (join ch 1, hdc count as ch-3 sp)—24 sc and 8 ch-3 spaces.

Round 3 (Slip st, ch 2, dc) in the join space (formed by the join ch 1, hdc), *ch 8, 2 dc in next ch-3 space; repeat from * around, ch 8: join with slip st in top of beginning ch-2—16 dc (eight 2-dc groups) and 8 ch-8 spaces.

Rounds 4 and 5 (Slip st, ch 2, dc) in space between beginning ch and next dc, *ch 7, 2 dc in space between sts of next 2-dc group; repeat from * around, ch 7; join with slip st in top of beginning ch-2—16 dc (eight 2-dc groups) and 8 ch-7 spaces).

Round 6 (Slip st, ch 2, dc) in space between beginning ch and next dc, *ch 4, insert hook in ch-8 space 3 rows below and work a sc drawing the ch-8 space and 2 ch-7 spaces of previous rounds together, picot, sc again in same space, ch 4 **, 2 dc in space between sts of next 2-dc group; repeat from * around ending last repeat at **; join with slip st in top of beginning ch-2—16 dc (eight 2-dc groups), 16 sc, 8 picots, and 16 ch-4 spaces.

Round 7 (Slip st, ch 2, dc) in space between beginning ch and next dc, *ch 9, 2 dc in space between sts of next 2-dc group; repeat from * around; join with ch 7, dc in top of beginning ch-2 (join ch 7, dc count as ch-9 space)—16 dc (eight 2-dc groups) and 8 ch-9 spaces.

Round 8 (Slip st, ch 2, dc) in the join space (formed by the join ch 7, dc), dc in next dc (top of beginning ch-2), *dc in next space between sts, dc in next dc, 2 dc in next ch-9 space (lower jaw made), ch 5 **, 2 dc in same ch-9 space, dc in next dc; repeat from * around ending last repeat at **; join with slip st in top of beginning ch-2—8 lower jaws and 8 ch-5 spaces.

Round 9 Ch 3 (counts as dc, ch 1), skip next dc, dc in next dc, *[ch 1, skip next dc, dc in next dc] twice (teeth made), ch 7 **, dc in next dc, ch 1, skip next dc, dc in next dc; repeat from *

around ending last repeat at **; join with slip st in 2nd ch of beginning ch-3—8 teeth and 8 ch-7 spaces.

Round 10 Ch 2, 2 dc in same st as join, *[dc in next ch-1 space, dc in next dc] twice, dc in next ch-1 space, 3 dc in next dc (upper jaw made), ch 5 **, 3 dc in next dc; repeat from * around ending last repeat at **; join with slip st in top of beginning ch-2—8 upper jaws and 8 ch-5 spaces.

Round 11 Ch 2, dc in same st as join, *dc in next dc, 3 dc in next dc, skip next 2 dc, Fpdc around next dc, skip next 2 dc, 3 dc in next dc, dc in next dc, 2 dc in next dc (nose made), ch 4 **, 2 dc in next dc; repeat from * around ending last repeat at **; join with slip st in top of beginning ch-2—8 noses and 8 ch-4 spaces.

Round 12 Ch 2, dc in next 2 dc, *ch 2, slip st in next 3 dc, slip st in space before next Fpdc, ch 2, Fpdc around next Fpdc, ch 2, slip st in space following Fpdc, slip st in next 3 dc, ch 2, dc in next 3 dc (eye base made), ch 5 **, dc in next 3 dc; repeat from * around ending last repeat at **; join with slip st in top of beginning ch-2—eye bases for 8 skulls and 8 ch-5 spaces.

Round 13 Ch 2, dc in next 2 dc, *dc in top of next ch-2, ch 6, dc in top of next ch-2, dc in next Fpdc, dc in top of next ch-2, ch 6, dc in top of next ch-2, dc in next 3 dc, ch 2, dc in next ch-5 space, ch 2 **, dc in next 3 dc; repeat from * around, ending last repeat at **; join with slip st in top of beginning ch-2.

Round 14 Ch 1, dc in next dc (beginning ch-1 and following dc count as first dc2tog), *dc in next 2 dc, 2 sc in next ch-6 space, dc in next 3 dc, 2 sc in next ch-6 space, dc in next 2 dc, dc2tog, ch 4, dc in next dc, ch 4 **, beginning in next dc work dc2tog; repeat from * around ending last repeat at **; join with slip st in first dc.

Round 15 Ch 1, beginning in next dc work dc2tog (beginning ch-1 and following dc2tog count as first dc3tog), *dc in next 7 sts, dc3tog, ch 6, 2 dc in next dc, ch 6 **, beginning in next dc

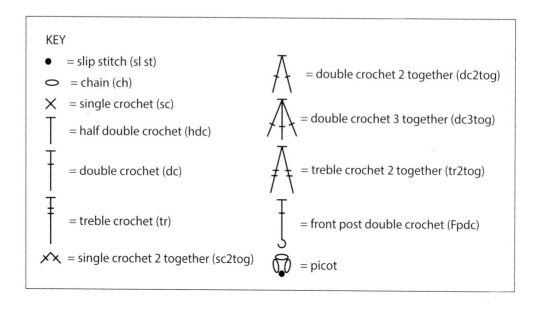

KEY

● = slip stitch (sl st)

◯ = chain (ch)

✕ = single crochet (sc)

T = half double crochet (hdc)

Ŧ = double crochet (dc)

Ŧ = treble crochet (tr)

✕✕ = single crochet 2 together (sc2tog)

⋀ = double crochet 2 together (dc2tog)

⋀ = double crochet 3 together (dc3tog)

⋀ = treble crochet 2 together (tr2tog)

Ŧ = front post double crochet (Fpdc)

= picot

work dc3tog; repeat from * around ending last repeat at **; join with slip st in first dc.

Round 16 Ch 1, beginning in same st as join work sc2tog, *sc in next dc, hdc in next 3 dc, sc in next dc, sc2tog, ch 10, 2 dc in space between sts of next 2- dc group **, ch 10, beginning in next dc, sc2tog; repeat from * around ending last repeat at **; join with ch 8, dc in first sc (join ch 8, dc count as ch-10 space)—8 skulls completed.

Round 17 Ch 10 (counts as dc, ch 8), *dc in next ch-10 space, ch 6, 2 dc in same ch-10 space, dc in next dc, dc in next space between sts, dc in next dc, 2 dc in next ch-10 space, ch 6 **, dc in same ch-10 space, ch 8; repeat from * around ending last repeat at **; join with slip st in 2nd ch of beginning ch-10—8 lower jaws, 8 ch-8 spaces and 16 ch-6 spaces.

Round 18 Slip st in first ch-8 space, ch 4 (counts as dc, ch 2), *(dc, ch 3, dc, ch 2, dc) in same ch-8 space, ch 7, skip next dc, dc in next dc, [ch 1, skip next dc, dc in next dc] 3 times, ch 7 **, dc in next ch-8 space, ch 2; repeat from * around ending last repeat at **; join with slip st in 2nd ch of beginning ch-4.

Round 19 Ch 6 (counts as dc, ch 4 here and throughout), skip next dc, sc in next ch-3 space, *ch 4, skip next dc, dc in next dc, ch 6, 3 dc in next dc, [dc in next ch-1 space, dc in next dc] twice, dc in next ch-1 space, 3 dc in next dc, ch 6 **, dc in next dc, ch 4, skip next dc, sc in next ch-3 space; repeat from * around ending last repeat at **; join with slip st in 2nd ch of beginning ch-6.

Round 20 Ch 6, tr2tog over same dc as join and next dc (skipping the 2 ch-sps between the dc sts), *ch 4, dc in same dc as last leg of tr2tog just made, ch 6, 2 dc in next dc, dc in next dc, 3 dc in next dc, skip next 2 dc, Fpdc around next dc, skip next 2 dc, 3 dc in next dc, dc in next dc, 2 dc in next dc, ch 6 **, dc in next dc, ch 4, tr2tog over last dc worked into and next dc; repeat from * ending last repeat at **; join with slip st in 2nd ch of beginning ch-6.

Round 21 Ch 6, *sc in space between legs of next tr2tog, ch 4, dc in next dc, ch 7, dc in next 3 dc, ch 2, slip st in next 3 dc, slip st in space before next Fpdc, ch 2, Fpdc around next Fpdc, ch 2, slip st in space following next Fpdc, slip st in next 3 dc, ch 2, dc in next 3 dc, ch 7 **, dc in next dc, ch 4; repeat from * around ending last repeat at **; join with slip st in 2nd ch of beginning ch-2.

Round 22 Ch 6, tr2tog over same dc as join and next dc, *ch 4, dc in same dc as last leg of tr2tog, ch 7, dc in next 3 dc, dc in top of next ch-2, ch 6, dc in top of next ch-2, dc in next Fpdc, dc in top of next ch-2, ch 6, dc in top of next ch-2, dc in next 3 dc **, ch 7, dc in next dc, ch 4, tr2tog over same dc and next dc; repeat from * around ending last repeat at **; join with ch 3, tr in 2nd ch of beginning ch-6 (joining ch 3, tr count as ch-7 space).

Round 23 Ch 6, *sc in next dc, ch 4, dc in space between legs of next tr2tog, ch 4, sc in next dc, ch 4, dc in next ch-7 space, ch 5, dc2tog, dc in next 2 dc, 2 sc in next ch-6 space, dc in next 3 dc, 2 sc in next ch-6 space, dc in next 2 dc, dc2tog, ch 5 **, dc in next ch-7 space, ch 4; repeat from * around ending last repeat at ** join with slip st in 2nd ch of beginning ch-6.

Round 24 Ch 6, tr2tog over same dc as join and next dc, *ch 4, dc in same dc as last leg of tr2tog just made, ch 4, tr2tog over same dc as last leg of tr2tog and next dc, ch 4, dc in same dc as last leg of tr2tog just made, ch 7, dc3tog, dc in next 7 sts, dc3tog **, ch 7, dc in next dc, ch 4, tr2tog over same dc and next dc; repeat from * around ending last repeat at **; join with ch 3, tr in 2nd ch of beginning ch-6.

Round 25 Ch 6, sc in next dc, *[ch 4, dc in space between legs of next tr2tog, ch 4, sc in next dc] twice, ch 4, dc in next ch-7 space, ch 6, sc2tog, sc in next dc, hdc in next 3 dc, sc in next dc, sc2tog, ch 6 **, dc in next ch-7 space, ch 4, sc in next dc; repeat from * around ending last repeat at **; join with slip st in 2nd ch of beginning ch-6.

Round 26 Ch 6 (counts as dc, ch 4), tr2tog over same dc as join and next dc, *ch 4, dc in same dc as last leg of tr2tog just made, [ch 4, tr2tog over same dc and next dc, ch 4, dc in same dc as last leg of tr2tog just made] twice, ch 4, dc in next ch-6 space, ch 9, dc in next ch-6 space, ch 4 **, dc in next dc, ch 4, tr2tog over same dc and next dc; repeat from * around ending last repeat at **; join with slip st in 2nd ch of beginning ch-6.

Round 27 Ch 1, sc in same st as join, *4 sc in next ch-4 space, sc in space between legs of next tr2tog, 4 sc in next ch-4 space, sc in next dc, ch 3, (tr, ch 3, tr) in space between legs of next tr2tog, ch 3, sc in next dc, 4 sc in next ch-4 space, sc in space between legs of next tr2tog, 4 sc in next ch-4 space, sc in next dc, 2 sc in next ch-4 space, ch 4, (tr, ch 4, tr) in next ch-9 space, ch 4, 2 sc in next ch-4 space **, sc in next dc; repeat from * around ending last repeat at **; join with slip st in first sc.

Round 28 Ch 1 (counts as hdc), hdc in next 2 sc, *sc in next 3 sc, picot, sc in next 2 sc, hdc in next 2 sc, dc in next sc, (3 dc, picot, 2 dc) in each of next 3 ch-3 spaces, dc in next sc, hdc in next 2 sc, sc in next 3 sc, picot, sc in next 2 sc, hdc in next 3 sc, dc in next 2 sc, (3 dc, picot, 2 dc) in next ch-4 space, (4 dc, picot, 3 dc) in next ch-4 space, (3 dc, picot, 2 dc) in next ch-4 space, dc in next 2 sc **, hdc in next 3 sc; repeat from * around ending last repeat at **; join with slip st in beginning ch-1.Fasten off.

FINISHING

Weave in ends. Block doily as desired. ●

AUNT LYDIA'S® Fashion Crochet size 3, Art. 182 available 100% Mercerized Cotton, 150yd/147m balls

japanese dahlia doily

Intermediate

MATERIALS

Yarn
• AUNT LYDIA'S® Crochet Thread, Fashion 3
• 1 ball each in 423 Maize

Hook
• Crochet hook, size E-4 (3.5mm), *or size to obtain gauge*

Notions
• Yarn needle

FINISHED MEASUREMENTS
Approximately 11"/28cm in diameter

GAUGE
Rounds 1–7 = 4"/10cm in diameter
CHECK YOUR GAUGE.
Use any size hook to obtain gauge.

SPECIAL STITCHES

5-dc shell (5 double crochet shell) Dc in first ch of next ch-5 space, [ch 1, dc in next ch of same ch-5 space] 4 times.

7-dc shell (7 double crochet shell) Dc in first ch of next ch-7 space, [ch 1, dc in next ch of same ch-7 space] 6 times.

9-dc shell (9 double crochet shell) Dc in first ch of next ch-9 space, [ch 1, dc in next ch of same ch-9 space] 8 times.

picot Ch 2, sc in 2nd ch from hook.

sc dec (single crochet decrease) [Insert hook in next ch-1 space and draw up a loop] twice, yarn over and draw through all 3 loops on hook.

DOILY

Round 1 (Right Side) Ch 2, sc in 2nd ch from hook, [ch 3, sc in same ch] 5 times; join with ch 1, hdc in first sc (counts as last ch-3 space)—6 sc and 6 ch-3 spaces.

Round 2 Sc around post of joining hdc, [ch 3, sc in next ch-3 space] 5 times; join with ch 1, hdc in first sc.

Round 3 Sc around post of joining hdc, [ch 4, sc in next ch-3 space] 5 times; join with ch 2, hdc in first sc (counts as last ch-4 space)—6 sc and 6 ch-4 spaces.

Round 4 Sc around post of joining hdc, [ch 3, (sc, ch 3, sc) in next ch-4 space] 5 times, ch 3, sc in next ch-4 space; join with ch 1, hdc in first sc—12 sc and 12 ch-3 spaces.

Round 5 Sc around post of joining hdc, [ch 4, sc in next ch-3 space] 11 times; join with ch 1, dc in first sc (counts as last ch-4 space)—12 sc and 12 ch-4 spaces.

Round 6 Sc around post of joining dc, [ch 5, sc in next ch-4 space] 11 times; join with ch 2, dc in first sc (counts as last ch-5 space)—12 sc and 12 ch-5 spaces.

Round 7 Sc around post of joining dc, [ch 5, sc in next ch-5 space] 11 times; join with ch 1, tr in first sc (counts as last ch-5 space).

Round 8 (Sc, ch 5, sc) around post of joining tr, [ch 4, (sc, ch 5, sc) in next ch-5 space] 11 times; join with ch 1, dc in first sc—24 sc, 12 ch-5 spaces and 12 ch-4 spaces.

Round 9 Sc around post of joining dc, ch 1, 5-dc shell in next ch-5 space, [ch 1, sc in next ch-4 space, ch 1, 5-dc shell in next ch-5 space] 11 times, ch 1; join with slip st in first sc—Twelve 5-dc shells and 12 sc.

Round 10 Sc in next ch-1 space, picot, *[sc in next ch-1 space, picot] 4 times **, sc dec, picot; repeat from * around, ending last repeat at **; insert hook in last ch-1 space and draw up a loop, insert hook in first sc, yarn over and draw loop through all loops on hook—60 picots.

Round 11 Ch 1, working behind sts of Round 10 in 5-dc shells of Round 9, slip st in first dc of first 5-dc shell, [ch 1, sc in next dc] 3 times, ch 7, skip last dc of same shell, *skip first dc of next shell, sc in next dc, [ch 1, sc in next dc] twice, ch 7, skip last dc of same shell; repeat from * around; join with slip st in first sc—12 ch-7 spaces and 36 sc.

Round 12 Slip st in next ch-1 space, sc in next sc, ch 1, 7-dc shell in next ch-7

japanese dahlia doily

space, [ch 1, skip next sc, sc in next sc, ch 1, 7-dc shell in next ch-7 space] 11 times, ch 1; join with slip st in first sc—Twelve 7-dc shells and 12 sc.

Round 13 Sc in next ch-1 space, picot, *[sc in next ch-1 space, picot] 6 times **, sc dec, picot; repeat from * around, ending last repeat at **; insert hook in last ch-1 space and draw up a loop, insert hook in first sc, yarn over and draw loop through all loops on hook—84 picots.

Round 14 Ch 1, working behind sts of Round 13 in 7-dc shells of Round 12, slip st in first dc of first 7-dc shell, ch 1, slip st in next dc, [ch 1, sc in next dc] 3 times, ch 9, skip last 2 dc of same shell, *skip first 2 dc of next shell, sc in next dc of same shell, [ch 1, sc in next dc] twice, ch 9, skip last 2 dc of same shell; repeat from * around; join with slip st in first sc—12 ch-9 spaces and 36 sc.

Round 15 Slip st in next ch-1 space, sc in next sc, ch 1, 9-dc

shell in next ch-9 space, [ch 1, skip next sc, sc in next sc, ch 1, 9-dc shell in next ch-9 space] 11 times, ch 1; join with slip st in first sc—Twelve 9-dc shells and 12 sc.

Round 16 Sc in next ch-1 space, picot, *[sc in next ch-1 space, picot] 8 times **, sc dec, picot; repeat from * around, ending last repeat at **; insert hook in last ch-1 space and draw up a loop, insert hook in first sc, yarn over and draw loop through all loops on hook—108 picots. Fasten off.

FINISHING
Weave in ends.•

AUNT LYDIA'S® Fashion Crochet size 3, Art. 182 available 100% Mercerized Cotton, 150yd/147m balls.

KEY

● = slip stitch (sl st)

⬯ = chain (ch)

✕ = single crochet (sc)

⊤ = half double crochet (hdc)

⊤ = treble crochet (tr)

✕✕ = single crochet decrease (sc dec)

✕0 = picot

⊤ = double crochet (dc)

❢ = insert hook in last ch-1 space and draw up a loop, insert hook in first sc, yarn over and draw loop through all loops on hook

party doily coasters

MATERIALS

Yarn
- AUNT LYDIA'S® Classic Crochet Thread, Size 10
- 1 ball each in 001 White (A), 397 Wasabi (B), 494 Victory Red (C), and 484 Myrtle Green (D)

Hook
- Steel crochet hook, size 7 (1.5mm), *or size to obtain gauge*

Notions
- Thread needle

FINISHED MEASUREMENTS

Approximately 6"/15cm in diameter

GAUGE

32 sts = approximately 4"/10cm in single crochet (sc).
CHECK YOUR GAUGE.
Use any size hook to obtain gauge.

SPECIAL STITCHES

join with sc Place a slip knot on hook, insert hook in indicated stitch, yarn over and draw up a loop, yarn over and draw through both loops on hook.
sc3tog (single crochet 3 stitches together) [Insert hook in next stitch, yarn over and pull up a loop] 3 times, yarn over and draw through all 4 loops on hook.

NOTES

1) Doily is worked in joined rounds with right side always facing.
2) Doily can be worked in any of 3 different versions. Versions differ only in the thread color used for each round.

DOILY – VERSION 1

With A, ch 4; join with slip st in first ch to form a ring.
Round 1 (Right Side) Ch 1, work 12 sc in ring; join with slip st in first sc—12 sc.
Round 2 Ch 1, 2 sc in each sc around; join with slip st in first sc—24 sc.
Round 3 Ch 4 (counts as dc, ch 1), dc in next sc, *ch 1, dc in next sc; repeat from * around, ch 1; join with slip st in 3rd ch of beginning ch-4—24 dc and 24 ch-1 spaces.
Round 4 Slip st in first ch-1 space, ch 3 (counts as dc), dc in same ch-1 space, 2 dc in each remaining ch-1 space around; join with slip st in top of beginning ch-3—48 dc.
Remove loop of A from hook, enlarge the loop so that it does not unravel and drop it to the wrong side of piece. Do not cut A. You will pick up and use A again later.
Round 5 With right side facing, join B with sc in any dc, 2 sc in next dc, *sc in next dc, 2 sc in next dc; repeat from * around; join with slip st in first sc—72 sc.
Fasten off B. Return dropped loop of A to hook.
Round 6 With A, slip st in closest sc of Round 5, ch 1, sc in same sc, *ch 9, skip next 11 sc, sc in next sc; repeat from * to last 11 sc, ch 9, skip last 11 sc; join with slip st in first sc—6 sc and 6 ch-9 spaces.
Round 7 Ch 1, sc in same st as join, (5 dc, ch 2, 5 dc) in next ch-9 space, *sc in next sc, (5 dc, ch 2, 5 dc) in next ch-9 space; repeat from * around; join with slip st in first sc—6 sc and 6 (5 dc, ch 2, 5 dc) groups.
Round 8 Ch 1, sc in same st as join, *sc in next 2 dc, dc in next 3 dc, (2 tr, ch 2, 2 tr) in next ch-2 space, dc in next 3 dc, sc in next 2 dc **, sc in next sc; repeat from * around ending last repeat at **; join with slip st in first sc—30 sc, 36 dc and 6 (2 tr, ch 2, 2 tr) groups (6 points).
Fasten off A.
Round 9 With right side facing, join C with sc in any ch-2 space, 2 sc in same ch-2 space. sc in each st to next ch-2 space, *3 sc in next ch-2 space, sc in each st to next ch-2 space; repeat from * around; join with slip st in first sc—108 sc.
Fasten off C.
Round 10 With right side facing, join A with sc in first sc of 3-sc group at

tip of any point, *ch 2, slip st in 2nd ch from hook (picot made), skip next sc, sc in next 7 sc, sc3tog **, sc in next 7 sc; repeat from * to last 6 sc ending last repeat at **, sc in last 6 sc; join with slip st in first sc—90 sc and 6 picot.
Fasten off A.

Round 11 With right side facing, join D with sc in sc immediately before any picot, *ch 4, skip picot, sc in next sc, ch 1, skip next sc, dc in next 3 sc, tr in next 5 sc, dc in next 3 sc **, ch 1, skip next 2 sc, sc in next sc; repeat from * to last 2 sc, ch 1, skip last 2 sc; join with slip st in first sc—78 sts, 12 ch-1 spaces, and 6 ch-4 spaces (2 sc, 6 dc, 5 tr and 2 ch-1 spaces between ch-4 spaces).

Round 12 Ch 1, sc in same st as join, *5 sc in next ch-4 space, sc in next sc, hdc in next ch-1 space, hdc in next 4 sts, dc in next st, 2 dc in next st, dc in next st, hdc in next 4 sts, hdc in next ch-1 space **, sc in next st; repeat from * around ending last repeat at **; join with slip st in first sc—126 sts (21 sts along each of 6 sides).
Fasten off D.

Round 13 With right side facing, draw up a loop of B in center sc of 5-sc group at tip of any point, ch 2 (counts as hdc), hdc in same st, hdc in next 5 sts, *2 hdc in next st, hdc in next 5 sts; repeat from * around; join with slip st in top of beginning ch-2—147 hdc.
Fasten off B.

Round 14 With right side facing, join C with sc in any hdc, sc in next 5 hdc, 2 sc in next hdc, *sc in next 6 hdc, 2 sc in next hdc; repeat from * around; join with slip st in first sc—168 sc.

Round 15 *Ch 2, slip st in 2nd ch from hook (picot made), skip next sc, slip st in next 2 sc; repeat from * around—56 picots.
Fasten off C.

DOILY – VERSION 2

Make same as Doily – Version 1, using A for Rounds 1–4, C for Round 5, A for Rounds 6–8, D for Round 9, A for Round 10, B for Rounds 11 and 12, C for Round 13, and D for Rounds 14 and 15.

DOILY – VERSION 3

Make same as Doily – Version 1, using A for Rounds 1–4, D for Round 5, A for Rounds 6–8, B for Round 9, A for Round 10, C for Rounds 11 and 12, D for Round 13, and B for Rounds 14 and 15.

FINISHING

Weave in ends. Gently steam press to block. •

AUNT LYDIA'S® Classic Crochet Thread, Size 10, Art. 154 available in white, ecru & natural 400yd/366m; solid color 350yd/320m; shaded color 300yd/274m balls.

KEY

- • = slip stitch (sl st)
- ⊂ = chain (ch)
- ✕ = single crochet (sc)
- ⊤ = half double crochet (hdc)
- ⊤ = double crochet (dc)
- ⊤ = treble crochet (tr)
- ⋀⋀ = single crochet 3 together (sc3tog)

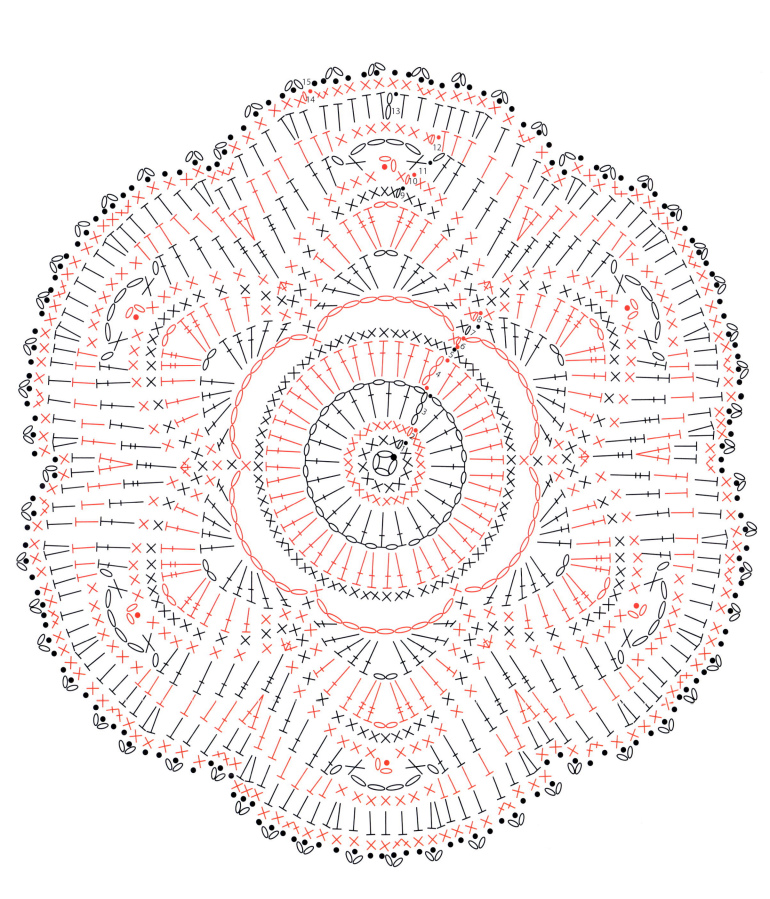

starshine doily

Intermediate

MATERIALS

Yarn
- AUNT LYDIA'S® Classic Crochet Thread, Size 10
- 1 ball in 423 Maize

Hook
- Steel crochet hook, size 7 (1.65mm), *or size to obtain gauge*

FINISHED MEASUREMENTS

Approximately 14"/35.5cm across

GAUGE

8 dc = 1"/2.5cm and 5 rows = 1"/2.5cm.
CHECK YOUR GAUGE.
Use any size hook to obtain gauge.

SPECIAL ABBREVIATIONS

fptr (front post treble) [Yarn over] twice, insert hook from the front side of the work to back and to front again around the post of the indicated stitch on a previous row; yarn over and pull up a loop (4 loops on hook), [yarn over and draw through 2 loops] 3 times.

trtr (treble treble) [Yarn over] 4 times, insert hook in next stitch, yarn over and pull up a loop (6 loops on hook), [yarn over and draw through 2 loops] 5 times.

edc (extended double crochet) Yarn over, insert hook in next stitch, yarn over and pull up a loop (3 loops on hook), yarn over and draw through 1 loop, [yarn over and draw through 2 loops] 2 times. This will give you a slightly longer than normal dc.

Triple Picot Ch 4, slip st into the front loop and front strand of the same stitch; ch 5, slip st into the same st and front loop of the first ch-4 loop made; ch 4, slip st into the same st and the front loops of the ch-4 loop and ch-5 loop.

2-tr cl (2-triple crochet cluster) [Yarn over] twice, insert hook in next stitch and pull up a loop, [yarn over and draw through 2 loops on hook] 2 times (2 loops remain on hook), [yarn over] twice, insert hook in same stitch and pull up a loop, [yarn over and draw through 2 loops on hook] 2 times, yarn over and draw through all 3 loops on hook.

3-dc cl (3-double crochet cluster) Yarn over, insert hook in indicated stitch and draw up a loop, yarn over and draw through 2 loops on hook (2 loops remain on hook), [yarn over, insert hook in same stitch and draw up a loop, yarn over and draw through 2 loops on hook] 2 times, yarn over and draw through all 4 loops on hook.

3-tr cl (3-triple crochet cluster) [Yarn over] twice, insert hook in next stitch and pull up a loop, [yarn over and draw through 2 loops on hook] 2 times (2 loops remain on hook), *[yarn over] twice, insert hook in same stitch and pull up a loop, [yarn over and draw through 2 loops on hook] 2 times*, repeat from * to *, yarn over and draw through all 4 loops on hook.

DOILY

Ch 5, slip st to form ring.

Round 1 Ch 2, 15 dc in ring, slip st into second ch of beginning ch-2—16 dc.

Round 2 Slip st around the post of the next dc, ch 7; *skip next dc, fptr in next dc, ch 4 *; repeat from * to * around, ending with a slip st into the third ch of the beginning ch-7—8 fptr; 8 ch-4 spaces.

Round 3 Slip st into ch-4 space, ch 2; 5 dc in same space; *ch 1, 6 dc in next ch-4 space *; repeat from * to * around, ending with hdc into the second ch of the beginning ch-2—48 dc; 8 ch-1 spaces.

Round 4 Ch 3, 4 tr in same space; *ch 6, skip next 6 dc, 5 tr in next ch-1 space *; repeat from * to * around, ending with a ch 3, edc into the third ch of beginning ch-3—40 tr; 8 ch-6 spaces.

Round 5 Ch 2, 3 dc in same space, dc in next tr, hdc in next tr, sc in next tr, triple picot in top of last sc made; slip st around base of triple picot just made, hdc in next tr, dc in next tr; *(4 dc, ch 1, 4 dc) in next ch-6 space; dc in next tr, hdc in next tr, sc in next tr, triple picot in last sc just made, slip st around base of triple picot just made, hdc in next tr, dc in next tr *; repeat

next picot on second adjoining motif, ch 1, slip st in top of last tr made, 2 tr) all in next ch 7 space, tr in next 2 tr tr, ch 1, sc in next picot on second adjoining motif, ch 1, slip st in top of last tr made, (edc, dc, hdc, 4 sc) all in next ch-6 sp.

Fourth Corner
Same as for Fourth Corner of Motif #2.

EDGING
Round 1 Starting on a short side of the doily with right side facing, attach B in the ch-5 picot at the top right corner; ch 10, tr in same picot.

Side 1 (Worked across four motifs)
*[Ch 4, sc in next picot] twice, ch 4, (tr, ch 4, tr) in next picot, [ch 4, sc in next picot] twice, ch 4 **, (tr, ch 4, tr) over next ch-5 picot motif joining; repeat from * twice, then from * to ** once; (tr, ch 7, tr) in next ch-5 picot on corner.

Side 2 (Worked across five motifs)
*[Ch 4, sc in next picot] twice, ch 4, (tr, ch 4, tr) in next picot, [ch 4, sc in next picot] twice, ch 4 **, (tr, ch 4, tr) over next ch-5 picot motif joining; repeat from * 3 times, then from * to ** once; (tr, ch 7, tr) in next ch-5 picot on corner.

Side 3
Same as for Side 1.

Side 4
*[Ch 4, sc in next picot] twice, ch 4, (tr, ch 4, tr) in next picot, [ch 4, sc in next picot] twice, ch 4 **, (tr, ch 4, tr) over next ch-5 picot motif joining; repeat from * 3 times, then from * to ** once; join with slip st in 3rd ch of beginning ch-10.

Round 2 Slip st in corner ch-7 space, ch 3, 12 tr in same space, 3 sc in next ch-4 space, *[7 tr in next ch-4 space, 3 sc in next ch-4 space] around to next ch-7 space **, 13 tr in ch-7 space, 3 sc in next ch-4 space; repeat from * twice, then from * to ** once; join with slip st in top of beginning ch-3. Fasten off. Weave ends in.

Round 3 With right side facing, attach A in back loop of 3rd ch of beginning ch-3 of Round 2; working in back loops only, ch 1, sc in same st, sc in next 3 tr, *ch-3 picot, [sc in next 3 tr, ch-3 picot] twice, sc in next 3 tr, skip next sc, sc in next sc, [skip next sc, sc in next 4 tr, ch-3 picot, sc in next 3 tr, skip next sc, sc in next sc, skip next sc] around to next corner **, sc in next 4 tr; repeat from * twice, then from * to ** once; join with slip st in first sc. Fasten off. Weave in ends. Block doily to size. •

AUNT LYDIA'S® Fine Crochet Thread, Size 20, Art. 181 available in 400yd/366m balls.

mandala doily

Intermediate

MATERIALS

Yarn
• AUNT LYDIA'S® Classic Crochet Thread, Size 10
• 1 ball each in 421 Goldenrod (A), 431 Pumpkin (B), 310 Copper Mist (C), 449 Forest Green (D), 672 Olive (E), 119 Violet (F), and 196 Cardinal Red (G)

Hook
• Steel crochet hook, size 3 (2.1mm), *or size to obtain gauge*

Notions
• Thread needle

FINISHED MEASUREMENTS

Approximately 14"/35.5cm in diameter

GAUGE

Rounds 1–5 = approximately 4"/10cm across. CHECK YOUR GAUGE.
Use any size hook to obtain gauge.

SPECIAL STITCHES

beg-Cl (beginning 3 treble crochet cluster) Ch 4, [yarn over] twice, insert hook in indicated stitch and pull up a loop, [yarn over and draw through 2 loops on hook] twice (2 loops remain on hook); [yarn over] twice, insert hook in same stitch and pull up a loop, [yarn over and draw through 2 loops on hook] twice, yarn over and draw through all 3 loops on hook.

beg-popcorn (beginning popcorn) Ch 3, work 4 dc in indicated stitch, drop loop from hook, insert hook from front to back in first dc of the 4 dc just made, return dropped loop to hook and draw through.

beg-tr3tog (beginning treble crochet 3 stitches together) Ch 4, *[yarn over] twice, insert hook in next st, yarn over and pull up a loop, [yarn over and draw through 2 loops on hook] twice; repeat from * once more, yarn over and draw through all 4 loops on hook.

Cl (3 treble crochet cluster) [Yarn over] twice, insert hook in indicated stitch and pull up a loop, [yarn over and draw through 2 loops on hook] twice (2 loops remain on hook); *[yarn over] twice, insert hook in same stitch and pull up a loop, [yarn over and draw through 2 loops on hook] twice; repeat from * once more, yarn over and draw through all 4 loops on hook.

dc2tog (double crochet 2 stitches together) [Yarn over, insert hook in next stitch, yarn over and pull up loop, yarn over, draw through 2 loops] 2 times, yarn over, draw through all 3 loops on hook.

Fpdc (Front post double crochet) Yarn over, insert hook from front side of work to back and to front again around post of indicated stitch, yarn over and pull up a loop (3 loops on hook), [yarn over and draw through 2 loops on hook] twice. Skip the stitch "behind" the Fpdc.

join with sc Place a slip knot on hook, insert hook in indicated stitch, yarn over and draw up a loop, yarn over and draw through both loops on hook.

picot Ch 3, slip st in 3rd ch from hook.

popcorn Work 5 dc in indicated stitch, drop loop from hook, insert hook from front to back in first dc of the 5 dc just made, return dropped loop to hook and draw through.

tr3tog (treble crochet 3 stitches together) *[Yarn over] twice, insert hook in next st, yarn over and pull up a loop, [yarn over and draw through 2 loops on hook] twice; repeat from * 2 more times, yarn over and draw through all 4 loops on hook.

SPECIAL TECHNIQUE

Adjustable Ring Wrap yarn into a ring, ensuring that the tail falls behind the working yarn. Grip ring and tail between middle finger and thumb. Insert hook through center of ring, yarn over (with working yarn) and draw up a loop. Work stitches of first round in the ring. After the first round of stitches is worked, pull gently on tail to tighten ring.

NOTES

1) Doily is worked in joined rounds with right side always facing.
2) Thread color is fastened off at the end of most rounds and a new color joined at beginning of next round.

mandala doily

DOILY

With A, make an adjustable ring.

Round 1 (Right Side) Beg-Cl in ring, [ch 5, Cl in ring] 7 times, ch 5; join with slip st in top of beginning ch – 8 clusters and 8 ch-5 spaces. Fasten off A and weave in ends.

Round 2 With right side facing, draw up a loop of G in any ch-5 space, (beg-popcorn, ch 3, popcorn) in same ch-5 space, *ch 3, (popcorn, ch 3, popcorn) in next ch-5 space; repeat from * around, ch 3; join with slip st in top of beginning ch—16 popcorns and 16 ch-3 spaces. Fasten off G and weave in ends.

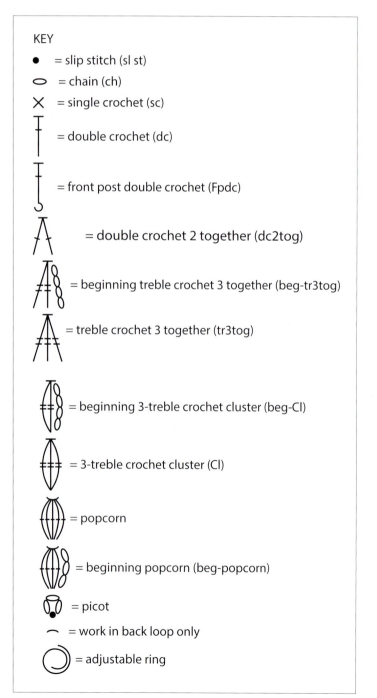

KEY

● = slip stitch (sl st)

◯ = chain (ch)

✕ = single crochet (sc)

 = double crochet (dc)

 = front post double crochet (Fpdc)

 = double crochet 2 together (dc2tog)

 = beginning treble crochet 3 together (beg-tr3tog)

 = treble crochet 3 together (tr3tog)

 = beginning 3-treble crochet cluster (beg-Cl)

 = 3-treble crochet cluster (Cl)

 = popcorn

 = beginning popcorn (beg-popcorn)

 = picot

 = work in back loop only

 = adjustable ring

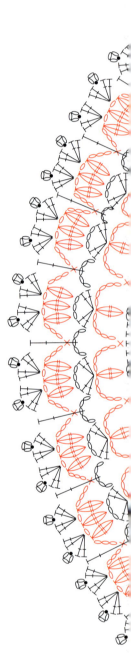

mandala doily

Round 3 With right side facing, draw up a loop of E in any ch-3 space, ch 8 (counts as dc, ch 5), dc in next ch-3 space, *ch 5, dc in next ch-3 space; repeat from * around, ch 5; join with slip st in 3rd ch of beginning ch—16 dc and 16 ch-5 spaces.

Round 4 Slip st in first ch-5 space, ch 3 (counts as dc), 5 dc in same ch-5 space, 6 dc in each of next 15 ch-5 spaces; join with slip st in top of beginning ch—Sixteen 6-dc groups. Fasten off E and weave in ends.

Round 5 With right side facing, join C with sc in first dc of any 6-dc groups, sc in next 5 dc, Fpdc around next dc of Round 3, *sc in next 6 dc of Round 4, Fpdc around next dc of Round 3; repeat from * around; join with slip st in first sc—16 Fpdc and sixteen 6-sc groups. Fasten off C and weave in ends.

Round 6 With right side facing, draw up a loop of F in back loop of any st, ch 3 (counts as dc), dc in back loop of each st around; join with slip st in top of beginning ch—112 dc. Fasten off F and weave in ends.

Round 7 With right side facing, draw up a loop of B in any st, beg-tr3tog, *ch 4, tr3tog; repeat from * around, skip last st; join with slip st in top of beginning ch—37 tr3tog and 37 ch-4 spaces. Fasten off B and weave in ends.

Round 8 With right side facing, draw up a loop of D in any ch-4 space, ch 3 (counts as dc), 4 dc in same ch-4 space, 5 dc in each ch-5 space around; join with slip st in top of beginning ch—Thirty-seven 5-dc groups. Fasten off D and weave in ends.

Round 9 With right side facing, join A with sc in first dc of any 5-dc group, sc in next 4 dc, Fpdc around next tr3tog of Round 7, *sc in next 5 dc of Round 8, Fpdc around next tr3tog of Round 7; repeat from * around; join with slip st in first sc—Thirty-seven 5-sc groups and 37 Fpdc. Fasten off A and weave in ends.

Round 10 With right side facing, draw up a loop of G in any Fpdc, (beg-Cl, ch 3, Cl) in same st, (Cl, ch 3, Cl) in each Fpdc around; join with slip st in top of beginning ch—74 clusters and 37 ch-3 spaces (thirty-seven (Cl, ch 3, Cl) groups). Fasten off G and weave in ends.

Round 11 With right side facing, draw up a loop of C in any ch-3 space, ch 3 (counts as dc) 4 dc in same ch-3 space, 5 dc in each ch-3 space around; join with slip st in top of beginning ch—Thirty-seven 5-dc groups. Fasten off C and weave in ends.

Round 12 With right side facing, join F with sc in first dc of any 5-dc group, sc in next 4 dc, dc in next space between (Cl, ch 3, Cl) groups of Round 10, *sc in next 5 dc of Round 11, dc in next

space between (Cl, ch 3, Cl) groups of Round 20; repeat from * around; join with slip st in first sc—Thirty-seven 5-sc groups and 37 dc. Fasten off F and weave in ends.

Round 13 With right side facing, draw up a loop of E in back loop of first sc of any 5-sc groups, ch 3 (counts as dc); working in back loops only, dc in next 4 sc, * ch 2, skip next dc, dc in next 5 sc; repeat from * to last dc, ch 2, skip last dc; join wth slip st in top of beginning ch—Thirty-seven 5-dc groups and 37 ch-2 spaces. Fasten off E and weave in ends.

Round 14 With right side facing, draw up a loop of B in any ch-2 space, beg-Cl in same ch-2 space, *ch 5, skip next 2 dc, sc in next dc, ch 5, skip next 2 dc, Cl in next ch-2 space; repeat from * to last 5-dc group, ch 5, skip next 2 dc, sc in next dc, ch 5, skip next 2 dc; join with slip st in top of beginning ch—37 clusters, 37 sc, and 74 ch-5 spaces. Fasten off B and weave in ends.

Round 15 With right side facing, draw up a loop of A in any Cl, ch 3 (counts as dc), (dc, ch 3, 2 dc) in same Cl, *ch 5, (2 dc, ch 3, 2 dc) in next Cl; repeat from * around, ch 5; join with slip st in top of beginning ch—37 (2 dc, ch 3, 2 dc) groups and 37 ch-5 spaces (between the groups). Fasten off A and weave in ends.

Round 16 With right side facing, draw up a loop of D in any ch-3 space, (beg-Cl, ch 1, Cl, ch 1, Cl) in same ch-3 space, *ch 3, sc in next ch-5 space, ch 3, (Cl, ch 1, Cl, ch 1, Cl) in next ch-3 space; repeat from * to last ch-5 space, ch 3, sc in last ch-5 space, ch 3; join with slip st in top of beginning ch—37 (Cl, ch 1, Cl, ch 1, Cl) groups, 37 sc, and 74 ch-3 spaces. Fasten off D and weave in ends.

Round 17 With right side facing, draw up a loop of E in first ch-1 space of any (Cl, ch 1, Cl, ch 1, Cl) group, ch 3 (counts as dc), picot, 2 dc in same ch-1 space, (2 dc, picot, 2 dc) in next ch-1 space, dc in next ch-5 space of Round 15, *(2 dc, picot, 2 dc) in each of next 2 ch-1 spaces of Round 16, dc in next ch-5 space of Round 15; repeat from * around; join with slip st in top of beginning ch. Fasten off E and weave in ends.

FINISHING
Weave in any remaining ends. ●

AUNT LYDIA'S® Classic Crochet Thread, Size 10, Art. 154 available in white, ecru & natural 400yd/366m; solid color 350yd/320m; shaded color 300yd/274m balls.